JOURNEY TO

MW00448398

THE PROCESS OF GROWTH AND CHANGE IN THE KINGDOM OF GOD

BY

STAN E. DEKOVEN

Journey to Wholeness: The Process of Growth and Change in the Kingdom of God

Copyright @ 2004 by Stan E. DeKoven, Ph.D.

ISBN: 1-931178-46-1

Published by

Vision Publishing

1520 Main Street, Suite C

Ramona, CA 92065

(760) 789-4700

www.visionpublishingservices.com

Unless otherwise noted, all Scripture references are from the New American Standard Bible or the King James.

First Printing: 1993

Second Printing: 1998

Third Printing: 2000

Fourth Printing: 2004

Printed in the United States of America

DEDICATION

The church has been under heavy fire. Men and women in God's family are recognizing the tremendous brokenness in lives and the need for Christ's healing restoration.

This book is dedicated to the men and women of God who, through their counseling and pastoral ministries, are assisting strugglers to become whole.

Further, it is dedicated to my wonderful family -- my wife Noreen, and my daughters, Rebecca and Rachel, the latter who have struggled along with me as I have continued to mature in the Lord.

Finally, I dedicate this work to my friend and mentor, the late Dr. Joseph Bohac, for starting me on my journey to wholeness.

May Father God be glorified.

Stan DeKoven, Ph.D.

TABLE OF CONTENTS

FOREWORD

"You can experience unconditional acceptance in your life."

"You are capable of manifesting unselfish love to others."

"You can overlook the faults of others, and see only their good."

Do these seem like lofty concepts, the impossible promises of some unobtainable vision?

They are not.

Rather, these promises embody the godly, biblical principles that Dr. Stan DeKoven shares as part of the vision God has given to the Body of Christ as we travel on the *Journey to Wholeness*.

If these ideals seem impossible to obtain, you are right -- they are -- in your own strength.

By yourself, you are absolutely incapable of giving unconditional acceptance, of offering unselfish love, and of seeing only the good in others.

But, when you walk the biblical path on the *Journey to Wholeness* with Christ by your side, all things, and all ideals, become possible and obtainable.

Dr. Stan DeKoven's message to the Body of Christ is that, through Christ, the Church can provide a safe place where the hurting members can be healed, a haven where the sinful members can be cleansed without condemnation, and a comforting home where the victims of addictions and abuse can become healthy and whole through God's restoring love.

But even in Christ, the *Journey to Wholeness* is not a road that can be traveled by accident!

Instead, it is a clearly detailed biblical path that is walked only by a deliberate decision, made by the collective Body of Christ, to unite together in love, and to purposely **DO** those things that Christ has commanded us to do.

No one ever became a world-class athlete without a stringent exercise program, discipline, and struggle.

So too, no Christian will ever become the compassionate, loving care-giver Christ intended him/her to be without first walking the required paths as outlined in this marvelous book.

Dr. DeKoven has written for you a Christian coach's guide to spiritual wholeness, giving you detailed biblical instructions on how to become all that Christ intends for you to be -- for yourself, and for others.

As you walk through the path on the *Journey to Wholeness* in this book, my prayer for you is that you grow in His love, that you mature in His compassion, and that you begin to manifest His living reality in your relationships with others.

In His service,

Michael Wourms
President
Christian Services Network

Introduction

Kingdom Living: Becoming Mature in Christ

For years, I have struggled in my Christian walk to arrive at a place where I could live my life according to biblical principles. Most people I have ministered to over the years share this same desire: to become all that God has created them to be. As I observed fellow believers, I would sometimes envy those who seemed to have it "all together," who seemed to live a life of "perfect" biblical balance.

Yet, what I have found, through years of counseling, is that despite outward appearances, most believers struggle with deep inner issues within their lives -- issues such as sin and lack of self-discipline. If you are struggling with these areas in your life, know that, from this moment on, you are not alone, or even that unusual.

As a Western Christian, I have tried hard to do things "right." I have punched all the right tickets on this train of life -- having completed a university education, obtained a modicum of success in my professional career, and have been faithful to the local church.

Despite these "right" steps, in many ways, I (seemingly) went in the wrong direction. In truth, I probably gave more emphasis to psychology than to Bible training and ministry. For many years, I thought I had made a mistake in the direction that I selected; yet, today I am convinced the Lord's hand was in it all.

Through my selection of psychology as a profession, God has allowed me to study human behavior, marriage and family counseling, as well as to prepare more fully for the ministry. You see, **the Lord knew the overall plan and purpose for my life** -- He knew the beginning, and He knows the end.

The same is true for your life!

God knows where you are now, and no matter how fragmented the parts of your life might seem at the moment, He knows where you are going -- and your life has a purpose!

I remember shortly after I was saved, my mom would encourage me to read the book of Proverbs. At an early age, I developed a hunger for God's Word and a hunger to know God in all of His fullness.

The primary scripture the Lord gave me as a young lad was Proverbs 3:5-6:

> *"Trust in the LORD with all your heart and lean not unto your own understanding. In all your ways acknowledge him and he will direct your path."*

I desired God's direction and guidance. I also desired wisdom to be able to help others who hurt and needed specialized ministry. After time, and growing in God, I began to study the field of psychology, developing a fascination as to why people do what they do, and what makes them function.

Through my university and graduate school training, I found there were not nearly as many concrete answers as there were nagging questions -- questions about why people do what they do, how dysfunctional patterns develop -- questions, questions, questions, but not always sufficient answers.

I sought God with all of my heart, asking Him to show me what model, what plan could be found in the Word that people could use to get to the place where they can be truly whole in the Lord. I found there were two keys toward experiencing inspired understanding:

1. Seek after God, and He will give you wisdom, and,
2. Be obedient to those things God shows you.

I did not always properly respond to the first key God gave me, the second one was frequently slow in coming. Herein lies a key to spiritual growth. The Living Bible says, *"Growth in wisdom comes from obeying his laws"* *(Psalm 111:10).*

As we obey God's guidance, putting His revelations into practice through obedience, we grow.

The book you are now holding in your hands is the result of my search, those revelations, **and God's guiding hand to help me grow. I honestly believe it is also the biblical plan and procedure for becoming what**

God wants you to be! The Lord has allowed me to synthesize this plan by first looking at the natural world, and then at the spiritual world, a process described in I Corinthians 15:46:

> *"Howbeit that was not first which is spiritual, but that which is natural; and afterward that which is spiritual."*

In this book, I liken the stages of psychological and physical development to those of a spiritual walk with God. Through a dynamic, interactive process between God, His word, and us, as led by the Holy Spirit, we can become all God created us to be. But to arrive at God's plan for our life, we must first understand the process, and then link the power of God into our lives to help our change occur.

My underlying assumption in writing this book is that **the key to complete wholeness in Christ is the application of clearly appropriated biblical principles which when consistently applied to our lives will lead to a change in lifestyle (what we call "true repentance").** The word "repentance" means "a change of thinking" that leads to a change in lifestyle.

Over the past few years there has been a renewal of interest in the Christian community for gaining a clearer understanding of the plan and purpose of God. Most have personalized this quest, seeking meaning, purpose, happiness and/or fulfillment through a genuine personal search. The search for truth, self-satisfaction, pain-free living and prosperity has led many of us into wilderness wanderings, doctrinal excess, relational turmoil, 12 steps to nirvana, faith fanaticism, or even worldly compromise. I do not mean to minimize the search. It has been, by and large, legitimate and heart-felt, even if at times directionless, leaving us sore and disappointed. Most Christians I know have become at times "burnt stones" in need of healing and cleansing, repentance and restoration, love, grace, and mercy. All of us who have been touched (and who can honestly say they have not?) by the madness of our materialistic culture, have needed a fatherly guide to bring us to the destination of our greatest fulfillment – being whatever God wants us to be.

It has been said that the Word of God is a road map, or at least a "lamp for our feet" (Ps. 119:105). Of course, this is completely true. The only difficulty with the map of God's Word (unlike most road maps, where the greatest difficulty is folding the silly thing), is that we do not always understand what it is saying nor how to systematically apply God's precious Word to our lives. There may be much we do know. But the fruitful application of the Word, for whatever reason, can be missing; leaving us hungry and thirsty, and at times bitter and desperate. We know that the keys to our successful walk with God must be contained in His Word. It is the task of every believer to conduct the difficult task of mining the nuggets for specific usage.

In times past, my goal for life has been quite different than what I discovered God's goal to be. Mine has been popularity, fortune, prestige, power, spirituality or anointing, etc. God's is far simpler and much less romantic...maturity. Maturity is defined as "having completed natural growth and development, ripe, the quality of being mature or fully developed" (Webster). Maturity from a biblical perspective can be defined in many ways, but is depicted as a process, not an event. It takes time and testing for one to become trained, equipped, restored, mature. A brief look at two of the primary biblical passages which speak profoundly of the maturation process will help us begin our journey together.

First, in Ephesians 4:11-16, we read the following:

> *"And He gave some as apostles, and some as prophets, and some as evangelists, and some as pastors and teachers, for the <u>equipping</u> of the saints for the work of service, to the building up of the body of Christ; until we all attain to the unity of the faith, and of the knowledge of the Son of God, to a mature man, to the measure of the stature which belongs to the fullness of Christ. As a result, we are not longer to be children, tossed here and there by waves, and carried about by every wind of doctrine, by the trickery of men, by craftiness in deceitful scheming; but speaking the truth in love, we are to <u>grow up</u> in all aspects into Him, who is the head, even Christ, from whom the whole body being fitted and held together by which every joint supplies, according to the proper working of each individual part, causes the growth of the body for the building up of itself in love."*

Christ has fully provided to His Church, from the least to the greatest member, special gifts. These gifts are actually people, men and women who have been called, selected, prepared and anointed (though they are not by any means perfect or better than the rest of us) by Jesus to actively assist in the building of the Body of Christ. They are to equip the saints (us) to become workers in the Body of Christ, His Church. The word "equip" (katartismos) means to complete furnishing, and comes from the word katartizo, which means essentially the same, but includes to mend or restore. This word is also found in Galatians 6:1, which speaks of the ministry of the mature, which is to restore or equip those who are fallen into sin. Thus, when we equip the saints we restore them and, likewise, when we restore them, we are equipping them.

It is important to note just what we are being equipped for: (service), that we know we have arrived (when our faith is unified), what we are to know or discern by experience (which is to become like Christ fully); and the results, which will be the putting away of childish things. Further, we will be stable in our life in Christ (not double-minded), able to tell truth from error and speak with living truth, by working together as brothers and sisters for God's greater good – the Kingdom of God.

Of course, to many this sounds almost impossible to achieve. Yet, this is the Biblical mandate, and will occur some day prior to the return of our Lord. (See Eph. 5:26-27).

A second picture of the progression of maturity, or journey to wholeness, can be seen in II Peter 1:1-11:

> *"Simon Peter, a bond-servant and apostle of Jesus Christ, to those who have received a faith of the same kind as ours, by the righteousness of our God and Savior, Jesus Christ: Grace and peace be multiplied to you in the knowledge of God and of Jesus our Lord; seeing that His divine power has granted to us everything pertaining to life and godliness, through the true knowledge of Him who called us by His own glory and excellence. For by these He has granted to us His precious and magnificent promises, so that by them you may become partakers of the divine nature, having escaped the corruption that is in the world by lust. Now for this very reason also, applying all diligence, in your faith supply moral excellence, and in your moral excellence, knowledge, and in your knowledge, self-control, and in your self-control, perseverance, and in your perseverance, godliness, and in your godliness, brotherly*

kindness, and in your brotherly kindness, love. For if these qualities are yours and are increasing, they render you neither useless nor unfruitful in the true knowledge of our Lord Jesus Christ. For he who lacks these qualities is blind or short-sighted, having forgotten his purification from his former sins. Therefore, brethren, be all the more diligent to make certain about His calling and choosing you; for as long as you practice these things, you will never stumble; for in this way the entrance into the eternal kingdom of our Lord and Savior Jesus Christ will be abundantly supplied to you."

Here, Peter, the great Apostle, states that the power to change, to grow, and to become what God desires has already been given to us. It comes to us through "true knowledge of Him," which is to be learned from the five-fold gifts to the Body of Christ, systematically presented and through our participation in His very nature (salvation) by His magnificent promises (His Word). Even though these are available and have been freely provided to us, we must take responsibility for our own journey in God. It is our responsibility as believers to press onward with diligence towards the goal of love (agape). Each of these steps in maturity could have a separate volume written about them. Each will be discussed here. The qualities Peter listed in this passage are the characteristics that lead to proper action or behavior. This must be possessed and increased for us to fulfill our destiny in God's kingdom.

The "how" of this process, of becoming all God has called us to be, is the process of maturity. Though the goal seems so far off, God's grace and the enduring application of His Word to our lives will bring us to our ultimate destination.

Finally, having taught these biblical principles in many nations over the past 10 years, I have seen the essential; it is a necessity to have a strong biblical foundation for these principles. The best, or most comprehensive passage outlining God's process for growth is found in 1 John 2:12-14. John, writing to the church at large, states,

"I am writing to you, little children, because your sins have been forgiven you for His name's sake. I am writing to you, fathers, because you know Him who has been from the beginning. I am writing to you, young men, because you have overcome the evil one. I have written to you, children, because

14

*you know the Father. I have written to you, <u>fathers</u>, because
you know Him who has been from the beginning. I have written
to you, <u>young men</u>, because you are strong, and the word of
God abides in you, and you have overcome the evil one."*

John describes three stages of spiritual growth; children, young men, and
fathers. Each stage, as will be discussed at length later, have certain needs
to be met and virtues to develop.

Children need to know that they are truly forgiven of their sins because of
the name of Jesus (Jesus' reputation requires he forgive when we seek
Him), and that we know who our "daddy" is. That is, we are not the child
of the world, the devil, religion, or any competing philosophy, but we are
the children of God. This knowledge provides the child of God
acceptance and security, the foundation for future growth.

In time, all children are to grow in responsibility, characterized by John as
young men. Young men must be overcomers (meaning they will face
battles mainly within the self) by having the Word of God abide (intimate
understanding of Christ and the Word) in them so that when temptations
and trials come, they can overcome as Christ did through the Word of
God.

Our goal is maturity, described by John as fathers. Fathers have a unique
relationship with Christ. They know him, not as children do, by
identification but by experience. As Paul stated, "That I may know him,
in the power of his resurrection, and in the fellowship of his suffering,
being conformed unto his death (Philippians 3:10)." Fathers know God's
works, but also his ways. They are not perfect, but sufficiently mature to
help others on their journey in Christ.

As you read this book, I trust you will be able to utilize this information to
bring about necessary changes within your own walk with God, and to
become truly the man or woman of God that you desire to be.

Dr. Stan DeKoven

SECTION ONE

THE INTIMATE RELATIONSHIP

CHILDREN

"I am writing to you, little children, because your sins have been forgiven you for His name's sake. I am writing to you, fathers, because you know Him who has been from the beginning. I am writing to you, young men, because you have overcome the evil one. I have written to you, children, because you know the Father. I have written to you, fathers, because you know Him who has been from the beginning. I have written to you, young men, because you are strong, and the word of God abides in you, and you have overcome the evil one."

1 John 2:12-14

CHAPTER ONE

IN THE BEGINNING: CHILDREN

THE DEVELOPMENT OF
AN INTIMATE RELATIONSHIP

Throughout most of my childhood, my parents had marital difficulties. The problems in their relationship were so serious that they separated on several occasions. As the middle of three children, I did not and could not understand the family dynamics of my parent's struggles.

To further confuse my childhood, our family had many other problems, especially in the area of finances. It seemed we never had sufficient money for family needs, although we always had an abundance of food.

To compensate for problems within our family, I worked very hard at being a positive part of the family; I wanted to be accepted, as all people do, to "fit in." Part of my "fitting in" was to eat the good food that was available.

In the process, I became quite a butterball! By the ninth grade, I stood about five-feet, six-inches tall, and weighed nearly 235 pounds. As my friends would say, "Stan plays the offensive line in high school -- the whole offensive line!"

Fortunately for me, I became a born again Christian in a small evangelical church in San Diego at the age of twelve. When I went to the altar for salvation, I waddled up, a young man filled with anger, lonely and scared, with pimples, a roll of fat around my middle, and a self-image that seemed to drag on the floor.

I only knew one thing when I went to that altar -- what I needed more than anything else was a Friend!

I needed someone who would love me just the way I was!

Although my parents gave me all the love they could, they were hurting in their own lives; I needed more than they were able to give. Something told me that Jesus Christ would know how to be that friend for me, that He would accept me just the way I was.

I remember when I stood up at that altar after having given my heart to the Lord Jesus Christ. Though I was still fat, still had pimples, still had family problems and other difficulties, I had one thing for certain...a new and special friend!

Further, I felt clean, forgiven, and I knew in my heart that this would be the beginning of something special.

As it says in II Corinthians 5:17, I became a new person in Christ!

> *"If any man be in Christ, he is a new creature: old things are passed away; behold all things are become new."*

At the time, I did not understand the ramifications of my decision from a theological viewpoint, but in my child-like faith, I knew that Jesus loved me.

The Hurts Continue

Despite this wonderful new relationship with Christ, I still continued to have many of the same hurts, angers and frustrations.

I went back to the same family.

But miraculously, the Lord soon began to move upon my mother, my sister, and brother's lives, and they all became born again (my mom was the first to be saved). Ultimately, my dad became born again as well. That experience made a significant difference in my family, but we were still not the most perfect human beings on planet Earth.

However, we were grateful we were all forgiven, and that we had a new love for one another.

Shortly after I became born again, I attended a church camp in the mountains outside of San Diego called "Pine Valley." It was there I received a definite call from God for full-time Christian service.

Although I received a powerful call from God, and knew that God wanted me for His service, that did not resolve all of my difficulties. I still struggled in certain areas of my Christian walk.

School was not always the easiest. Issues of morality were constantly present, especially since I was as sexually tempted as most young men. During my high school years I struggled with wanting so much to be accepted by my peers that I flirted with a worldly lifestyle. To further complicate my life, I still did not have anywhere near the perfect home environment that I thought we would have when we became believers.

The older I became, the more the simplicity of life that I remembered as a child disappeared. Some serious questions for the Lord began to emerge. I had read and studied His Word in a compulsive style (as was my nature). As I read, I believed God wanted me to be perfect.

Further, He had the power to bring solutions to my problems. He wanted to meet all of my needs.

Yet, the more that I tried to grow in God, the more distant from Him I seemed to be. This led me to seeking, from a position of desperation, a more intimate relationship with God.

I began to ask questions of various people regarding my need for a deeper walk. I remember talking to my pastor and asking, "Pastor, what do I need to do to be what God wants me to be?"

His simple answer was profound, and will be discussed in detail later in this book.

I knew that I needed to develop an intimate relationship with my God, I sought that with all of my heart just as many other Christians do. It is a common experience for others, as well as myself, that the closer they come to the Lord, the more the issues of life that are not pleasing to God become apparent, and need to be confronted.

In the process our walk with God becomes even more difficult.

This seemingly contradictory set of conclusions has led me to do the research that has produced this book. I was convinced that there must be solutions to the problems of growth to maturity that I desperately wanted, but seemed so evasive. Of course, the answers were in Scripture, and the power to become God's best is available through the Holy Spirit, but the ability to understand and activate these truths eluded me...a common reality of God's children.

CHAPTER TWO

DEVELOPING A RELATIONSHIP WITH GOD

Before going into our psychological and physical development as it relates to our spiritual development and growth in God, it is important to understand some basic principles regarding our relationship with the Lord.

Religion does not enable us to have a relationship with God. A relationship with God establishes religion.

As with any worthwhile relationship, the process of growing to know each other, then to experience closeness, then love -- takes time. Healthy relationships breed the desire to please one another, not out of fear or condemnation, but out of true love which is received and given.

When we come to know Christ as our Lord and Savior, our personality is not forfeited for a relationship with God. In fact, our different personalities are what make us unique and precious to God, and He only desires for us to have those personalities bloom.

No matter how hard we might try to do it, most of us will admit we are unable to love people unconditionally, to be totally unselfish, to be all-knowing in how to treat one another.

What we must forfeit in a relationship with God is this attitude of self-perfection. We cannot reach perfection in our own strength.

God, through His relationship with us, wants to develop our natural abilities, as well as our spiritual giftings, using both areas to help develop us into all He desires us to be.

Since no two people are alike, our natural talents are different; our weaknesses and strengths are different. So this process of relationship with God, in becoming mature and whole in Him, will be slightly different for each of us.

Yet, the process is always the same, because Jesus Christ does not change.

"Jesus Christ is the same yesterday and today and forever"
(Hebrews 13:8, NIV).

Sin Separates

The initial sin, which came into the world because of the fall of man, severed man's ability to have an intimate relationship with God, because man's own guilt and self-condemnation caused him to run from God (Genesis 3:8-13).

That process of separation still happens in your natural life today. When one spouse does something the other does not approve of, the relationship becomes marred due to guilt and self-condemnation.

God never abandoned man after he sinned. Even in the Garden of Eden, God actively sought after Adam for fellowship with him, only to find him hiding in guilt and shame.

> *"And they heard the voice of the LORD God walking in the garden in the cool of the day: and Adam and his wife hid themselves from the presence of the LORD God amongst the trees of the garden" (Genesis 3:8).*

Adam attempted to defend himself by projecting the blame for his sin onto God, then Eve, in turn, blamed the serpent.

> *"And the man said, The woman whom thou gavest to be with me, she gave me of the tree, and I did eat. And the LORD God said unto the woman, What is this that thou hast done? And the woman said, The serpent beguiled me, and I did eat" (Genesis 3:12, 13).*

The condition of man without Christ is one of isolation, separation from God, without hope in a lonely world. To eradicate sin, and the resulting guilt, shame, and anxiety experienced because of sin, God asked His only Son, Jesus, to accept the punishment for every wrong man has ever committed, or ever will commit.

Jesus accepted the responsibility, and became flesh.

Alive.

Vibrant -- given by God to mankind to be sacrificed for man's sake.

> *"Looking unto Jesus the author and finisher of our faith; who for the joy that was set before him endured the cross, despising the shame, and is set down at the right hand of the throne of God" (Hebrews 12:2).*

God allowed Jesus to become man so that He could fully experience His own creation, and then free man from self-condemnation and shame (a form of bondage which results from man recognizing his shortcomings.) But when man views his shortcomings in the light of what Jesus did, the process leads to peace, and the ability to grow in God.

The purpose of salvation is to <u>reconcile and restore right relationship</u> between God and man!

God did not reconcile and restore man so that He could give him a list of rules and regulations, do's and don'ts, that He knows man could not keep. God would not hold man in eternal bondage to guilt and shame. Sadly, many today fear that God's plan was devised so He could squash humans as a bug at life's end.

That notion is nonsense.

God loves each and every one of His creations more than man could ever love himself or any other person!

The Lord says He is our Father, and we are His children. He desires to reunite men with Himself for eternal fellowship.

Jesus lived a perfect life for all mankind, and accepted punishment in our place. In essence, when Jesus took man's place on the cross, it afforded man the opportunity to take his place in heavenly places with Christ.

> *"And (God) hath raised us up together, and made us sit together in heavenly places in Christ Jesus" (Ephesians 2:6).*

Our Free Choice

Jesus rose from the dead and presented Himself blameless before God on our behalf. Yet, God will never force His will on man, just as He would never force one person to love another.

God simply gives men the good news.

And the choice.

To accept Him, or reject Him.

> *"For God so loved the world, that he gave his only begotten Son, that whosoever believeth in him should not perish, but have everlasting life" (John 3:16).*

This scripture tells us that all mankind has a choice to accept or reject God, and based upon that decision, eternal life or judgment will be faced.

> *"And as it is appointed unto men once to die, but after this the judgment" (Hebrews 9:27).*

Those who have accepted the work of Jesus for their lives will not come under that great judgment, for their names have been written in the Lamb's Book of Life.

> *"And I saw a great white throne, and him that sat on it, from whose face the earth and the heaven fled away; and there was found no place for them. And I saw the dead, small and great, stand before God; and the books were opened: and another book was opened, which is the book of life: and the dead were judged out of those things which were written in the books, according to their works. And the sea gave up the dead which were in it; and death and hell delivered up the dead which were in them: and they were judged every man according to their works. And death and hell were cast into the lake of fire. This is the second death. And whosoever was not found written in the book of life was cast into the lake of fire" (Revelation 20:11-15).*

Jesus has already been judged and willingly condemned in our place!

Because of the death, burial, and resurrection of Jesus Christ, we have life and hope. He is interceding as man's High Priest at the right hand of the Father for us today.

> *"Seeing then that we have a great high priest, that is passed into the heavens, Jesus the Son of God, let us hold fast our profession. "For we have not an high priest which cannot be touched with the feeling of our infirmities; but was in all points tempted like as we are, yet without sin" (Hebrews 4:14,15).*

Jesus wants all men to become fully what God created them to be.

God desires to restore all things back to mankind so they can be whole and complete in Him.

The first step in the process of learning to walk with God into wholeness comes through the development of an intimate relationship with God, through His Son, Jesus Christ.

In the following chapters, both the psychological and spiritual developmental processes are presented, as an example of the process of development of our intimate relationship with God.

ERIKSONS
8 stages

CHAPTER THREE

THE NATURAL PROCESS

In the beginning of physical life, humans are totally dependent upon their care-givers for survival.

I remember so well when my precious daughters were born. Karen, my lovely wife, and I had such anticipation! We knew we were going to have the most beautiful children God had ever allowed to come into the world. We knew we would be good parents, for we had read all the "right" books and studied all the "right" things.

Of course, we were naive.

I assumed, just as in the movies, when our children were born they would be presented to us "without spot or wrinkle," cleaned and pressed, ready for cuddling.

Oh, was I surprised!

When my children were born, each appeared to be a wet, wrinkled mess of flesh. Their heads were oblong; almost from the first seconds in the world they seemed to do nothing but scream, cry, demand attention, eat and wet.

But, despite that initial shock, we were glad they were ours. Glorious, precious, helpless bundles of joy and quite a significant responsibility.

Because God is our heavenly Father, when we first come into His family, He sees us in much the same way we see our own children -- as glorious, precious, helpless bundles of joy. He knows we are totally dependent, helpless, and needy as we begin our spiritual journeys.

The First Stage

The first stage of natural development through childhood parallels the new, spiritual life in Christ.

What a bundle of potential we are!

And, what a mess!

From the first day of birth, children, and new Christians, tend to be quite demanding. Although we all have slightly different temperaments, we all cry, demand attention, and want to have our needs met <u>immediately</u>.

Children frequently disturb our sleep patterns with a 2:00 a.m. wake-up call. They often leave messes for us to clean up as reminders of their presence.

As we look at the natural world, as studied by child development specialists, psychologists, and social workers, we begin to see some specific patterns in children's behavior that can be directly applied to the spiritual world.

For example, just as babies are born into the natural world totally <u>dependent</u>, without the ability to fend for themselves, so it is with the new convert.

Natural Stages of Growth

Many developmental theories provide insight into our process of natural growth. For the sake of our study, and for brevity, Erik Erikson's 8 Stages of Psycho-Social Development has been chosen for illustration.

There are stages of psychological and physiological growth which are specifically pertinent to a spiritual walk in God.

Of Erikson's eight stages of "Psycho-Social Development," the first six are the most pertinent. Although the patterns are not perfectly aligned, you can see from the natural world patterns of our spiritual walk in God. These stages, presented ever so briefly, are provided as a picture of our growth in Christ.

Stage One: Trust Versus Mistrust

0-2 Years Old

Erik Erickson describes the first stage of our initial coming into the world as a stage of trust versus mistrust.

This first stage of initial bonding, which occurs between the parent and the child, is most essential. This bonding is of primary importance to the survival of the infant. Children who do not receive the initial love and affection they need, although their physical needs may be met, can still fail to grow and become viable (healthy) children.

During initial bonding, it is vital for children to learn trust, gaining a sense that their world is a safe place to be. If they do not receive a foundation of trust, they develop mistrust, which will undermine their process of growth.

The reports of the deplorable conditions in the Romanian orphanages have shocked the entire world. Fully one-third of these children have AIDS, and as many as one-half suffer from hepatitis B and malnutrition. The orphanages are so understaffed that often there is only one attendant for twenty to thirty little children. As a result, these tiny children are left psychologically malnourished, forced to rock themselves in cold iron cribs instead of being rocked in the loving arms of a caring mother. The world health community has discovered a shocking fact - these neglected children are dying in ever-increasing numbers from a disease no doctor can diagnose: a lack of love – known medically as a failure to thrive!

Next to AIDS, the leading cause of death in these Romanian orphans is a lack of love, a lack of attention, a lack of human contact!

Those neglected children who do survive are destined, without serious intervention, to live lives of pain and despair.

Stage Two: Autonomy Versus Shame

Ages 2-3

The second stage, as developed by Erickson, corresponds with (approximately) ages two through three, known as the stage of autonomy versus shame.

During this period, toddlers begin to move about and explore their world. They also begin the process of separation and individuation, becoming more autonomous and mobile in their environment. This season of development can be most problematic for many parents because children learn to say "no" as a natural response to almost any request.

Most parents recognize this stage as "the terrible two's."

As parents, it is important to allow children to explore their world and to try new things. But, they must also be protected from hurting themselves. If we do not allow the expression of a certain amount of autonomy, issues of shame will emerge. When parents constantly say, "That's a bad boy," or "What a naughty girl you are," the shamed child begins to develop a poor self-image, thwarting their growth towards maturity.

It has been said by many mental health professionals that the `90s were characterized as the age of the 12-step group. Frankly, it continues into the 21st century. The 12-step movement, deriving from Alcoholics Anonymous, is designed as a self-help recovery program for compulsive/addictive disorders. Researchers have found the core ingredient of compulsive/addictive problems is shame, which is developed in dysfunctional families. More than guilt, which is a feeling of self-condemnation for the breaking of a moral or societal rule, shame is a sense that I not only do wrong - **I am** inherently wrong or flawed.

Shame is the expression of failure **in us** - a violation of our own standards. It puts us under self-judgment. Shame often reflects itself as embarrassment, self-condemnation, self-hatred, defensiveness, fear, and hiding.

The opposite of shame is living without condemnation. God accepts us for who we are, and the answer to shame is the experience of being adopted in Christ, where we receive a new identity, a new image, where there is acceptance without condemnation.

In Romans, especially in chapters 5-8, the Bible clearly shows how our identity as Christians is rooted and established in Christ.

In compulsive and addictive behavior, self-centeredness is one of the main maladies that must be conquered. It is at the cross, and only at the cross, where God can cut across our will and destroy self-centeredness, replacing it with Christ as the center of our identity.

People in recovery have difficulty setting boundaries for themselves – manifested as co-dependent relationships. They have difficulty determining the difference between their own feelings, problems, and responsibilities and those of others. As a result, they pick up and absorb other people's feelings, draining the other person. Usually, as these people experience adulthood, their own self is so battered that they rely on others for their boundaries.

It is vital for parents to learn to correct or discipline through love, not condemnation, and to help children develop healthy boundaries. Pretense, fear, playing psychological games - all have to be eliminated.

Parents need to learn to set boundaries without trying to overly control their child. The goal in stage two is to create a loving, nurturing, healthy atmosphere that makes the child want to be together with the parent. To do this, the parent must be Christ-like, that is, accepting and loving of the child, without radiating condemnation or extreme criticism when the child fails to perform to the parental standard.

Children develop weak or non-existent personal boundaries if they are emotionally or physically abused, neglected or abandoned. In such an upbringing, the very love of being, or identity, is marred, leaving a sense of helplessness. This can be corrected in later life, but how much better to develop healthy autonomy through loving discipline and appropriate boundaries.

Stage Three: Initiative Versus Guilt

Ages 4-5

The next stage corresponds with ages of four to five, the stage of initiative versus guilt. This is a time when children try many new things. They are exploring symbols of language and thought, and are attempting to understand their world more clearly. They want to please Mom and Dad in everything they do.

The naturally curious child wants to try all things new. If the initiative is thwarted or overly coerced and punished, children can develop an acute sense of guilt.

If the four-year-old decides to help Mommy by washing dishes, and makes a mess on the kitchen floor, it is important that Mom tells her "thank you" for wanting to help, and then patiently explain what the child can do to avoid a mess the next time. It is important for the parents to learn to offer solutions instead of personal condemnation.

Stage Four: Industry Versus Inferiority

Ages 6-12

The next stage is industry versus inferiority. This stage corresponds with the ages of six through twelve. In the beginning of this stage children will make mud pies and present their **gifts** to Mom and Dad to show them how wonderful they are.

Parents who are sensitive to their children will gladly accept these gifts, and encourage them to try new things. In doing so, they develop the children's skills in many areas.

Those who do not encourage, but instead over-criticize their children, or reject their gifts, can cause an extreme sense of inferiority to develop in the children. The children learn to believe that they are not good enough to please Mommy and Daddy, creating an internal sense of worthlessness.

It should be noted that this stage corresponds with early educational experiences, where success and accomplishment (industry) becomes so important. A strong foundation of success at this stage opens the future, but failure to read, socially relate, etc. can lead to a sense of personal inferiority.

Stage Five: Identity Development Versus Role Confusion

Ages 12-18

In the adolescent stage, we see conflicts emerge between identity development versus role confusion.

It is important to remember that adolescence is not a disease; it is a time of the solidification of the question, "Who am I and how do I fit into the world?" Youth are asking questions like "How do I relate with my family, with my school, and with my friends?"

If identity is not solidified, a sense of confusion can develop, a feeling that, "I do not matter in this stupid world. I don't know who I am, or what I am supposed to be."

As the adolescent role in our society becomes increasingly difficult for young people to comprehend, some are selecting suicide as an alternative to living. Problems are blown completely out of the "normal" proportions adults have developed through the benefit of time and experience. That is why an adolescent may hurt himself or herself, who suddenly acts out because they were a straight A student who suddenly earned a B, or because they failed to make the cheerleading squad. Adolescents identify themselves almost totally as "A-Student" or "Cheerleader," and when those identities fail them, they become "failures."

Poor identity development, and especially inadequate bonding between the child of either sex and the father, can open the door to the potential development of a homosexual choice.

35

Stage Six: Intimacy Versus Isolation

Ages 19-35

Intimacy is the goal of this stage where marriage and family issues, and solving the problem of loneliness, and vocational choice is made.

In our day there seems to be a strong fear of intimacy; of experiencing close contact in various activities that are deep and personal. Intimate experiences can come from a variety of encounters, not just in the sexual arena (where it is traditionally spoken about). There can be intimate social contact, intellectual and emotional experiences, and even be experienced in recreational or spiritual settings.

Intimacy is something we all need to experience, which is a feeling of closeness and understanding between two or more people. This is especially true in a world where we are increasingly isolated from our neighbors, our fellow workers, or church members.

For many, especially men, sex and intimacy seem to be almost inseparable. Eventually, men need to learn to foster intimate relationships which are non-sexual, simply involving the sharing of life. Small Christian prayer groups often produce this "safe" intimacy which involves deep sharing without sexual overtones.

Some unpleasant behavior patterns may surface to avoid intimacy: gossip, blaming, punishing, fighting, judging, and self-pity. To develop an intimate relationship between a husband and wife involves a oneness of the spirit, soul, and body - in that order. Oneness in the spirit comes from a couple turning to the Lord for their security and significance. Oneness in the soul means a commitment to minister to each other's needs rather than manipulating the other spouse to the desired action or activities.

Finally, true body oneness follows. It is especially meaningful because that relationship involves the spirit and soul, as well as the body.

These first six stages are the most important, but we should be aware of the other two stages.

Stage Seven: Productivity Versus Stagnation

Ages 35-65

In this stage, adults learn how to accomplish goals in life.

Stage Eight: Ego Integrity Versus Despair

Age 65 up

In this stage, the cycle of life will be completed in either joy or bitterness.

Remember these natural stages are used here as a metaphor to illustrate the principles of growth in our spiritual walk. We now attempt to make spiritual application loosely based on these developmental principles.

CHAPTER FOUR

THE SPIRITUAL APPLICATIONS

When I was first saved, I was like a kid in a candy store. Just like a child, I wanted to taste everything in the jars; I wanted to taste everything pertaining to the things of God.

I had so many questions.

To many people, I must have seemed like a nuisance. Most new Christians are very much like children, wanting to know everything they can learn about the things of God. Most of the questions they have relate to "Why?"

"Why does God let people die from hunger?"

"Why didn't God hear my prayers when I was unsaved?"

"Why didn't I ever hear about the Holy Spirit before?"

When they are told to do things, the answer young children frequently give is "No."

That is the way with new babes in Christ.

As a child begins to grasp that he or she is a unique individual human being with strengths and weaknesses, the process of separation and individuation begins, and the development of personal power and self-esteem starts.

The initial stages of natural and Christian childhood are characterized by total dependency, but eventually, as Christians begin to grow, they recognize they have some personal responsibility for their own growth.

New Christians, if given a nurturing environment, will begin to develop a sense of trust - both in the Lord and in the Body of Christ. They will join various activities in the Church, and willingly help when asked.

Shortly after that initial phase of bonding to the Body of Christ, there begins an initial separation and individuation.

This is similar to normal child development.

This phase of childhood development can be very problematic (as most parents would recognize). In the last chapter, we called it "the terrible two's," a time that challenges both the children and the parents.

In spiritual terms, this stage occurs when young Christians begin to have enough basic knowledge in their Christian walk that they become capable of independent movement and Christian development. As a result, they begin to question their teachers, stating things such as, "I don't agree with that."

In the natural world, we can make grievous errors with our children if we give them too much freedom or responsibility. If the responsibility is more than the children can handle, they can become overwhelmed and discouraged, and could even inflict harm upon themselves.

Every father wants to see his children eventually be able to drive themselves, as responsible adults, to various functions in the family car. But, no sane father would give his three-year-old child the car keys to a Corvette and say, "Hey kid, go enjoy yourself."

The same prudence must be exercised with baby Christians.

As more mature Christians, we must be careful spiritual parents in the training and the development of our children. Many young Christians leave the Church too early, attempting to do things in God before they are ready. We must be careful not to put young Christians too quickly into teaching positions, counseling positions, or other key responsibilities in a church.

Remember, just because someone is a doctor, a lawyer, a capable housewife, or a nurse, does not mean that person will be a capable Christian teacher as soon as they are born again! Like any natural child, there must be a time of slow and careful development before heavy responsibility is placed upon them.

Just as earthly children can have a difficult childhood because of incomplete parenting, so spiritual children may also have problematic childhoods because of inadequate times of spiritual training.

The Apostle Paul warned that only mature men and women should take positions of leadership within the local church (I Timothy 2:2).

As with new children, new Christians need to go through the natural growth process of becoming what they are supposed to be. They have to learn trust, autonomy, initiative, and industry to develop a full identity of who they are in God.

Encourage Independence

In the spiritual development of new Christians, it is necessary to give them time and the proper parenting ingredients to allow growth to occur - so they can become conformed to the image of Christ. To do so, they must be encouraged to develop from a place of total dependency to independence, with the eventual goal of interdependence as full members of the Body of Christ.

As natural children begin to exhibit signs of autonomy and independence, they will still require care, nurturing and close supervision as they grow. Likewise, it is the responsibility of the local church to see that the new Christians receive the same nurturing.

It is essential, as with natural children, that young Christians be given close and careful supervision, loving care and discipline, so they might grow effectively in God. This will be outlined more fully as we deal with the primary stages of spiritual growth.

As the new Christian develops, the same emphasis must be placed upon positive reinforcement as opposed to the "bad boy," "naughty girl" method of correcting. I have heard perfectly well-intentioned, mature Christians shatter the fragile ego of a new Christian by some careless remark such as, "I can't believe it. I thought doctors were supposed to be smart, and yet you don't even know anything about the Holy Spirit!"

Christ's Model - Discipleship

Our development is a process commanded and modeled by Jesus. Further, it was modeled specifically in His relationship with His disciples. He spent nearly three years with them before He sent them out to minister.

Jesus would not have commanded us to become whole and complete if He did not believe we had the power to become so through the Holy Spirit working in us.

The process Jesus created to develop these brand-new babes in Christ to become what God wanted them to be is called "discipleship."

To become a disciple of Christ, the new Christian must move from a position of being in total darkness (which they were before salvation), to the total light of God.

Only through God can this be accomplished. God has a process outlined within His Word that all Christians must traverse to become fully equipped for effective service. The Christian's responsibility is to be willing to go through this biblical process, to yield to the Lord, so they can develop properly through the natural stages of growth.

As stated above, the first stage is the development of an intimate relationship with God. Jesus demonstrated how to do this through His life and work with His disciples. Paul stated that young Christians were like babies who need to be fed the milk of the Word.

> *"I gave you milk to drink, not solid food; for you were not yet able to receive it. Indeed, even now you are not yet able." (I Corinthians 3:2).*

Jesus desires for His children to move beyond the level of being totally dependent or spoon fed. We all begin with milk and baby food. But eventually, God desires for all men to mature to the point where they can eat and digest the meat of His Word, to grow strong in the Lord and His power.

It will be seen, as we process through this typological teaching that just as babies grow and change to become responsible adults, we too can become all God created us to be as we, with courage, walk through our spiritual journey.

The first stage in that spiritual growth process is to develop a fully intimate relationship with Jesus Christ. Let's look at how.

CHAPTER FIVE

DEVELOPING THE
INTIMATE RELATIONSHIP

The Lord Jesus came into a dark world filled with sin and its results. Yet, Jesus was a man who was comfortable with sinners, people who hurt, people like you and me. He did not seem to care how wanting or worthy we were. He gave Himself completely for our salvation. How profoundly God the Father must have desired our love to have sacrificed so great a gift!

Throughout the Word of God there are examples of the kind of intimate relationship Jesus shared with His Father. From Adam and Eve, to David and Jonathan, to Ruth and Boaz, and especially in the life of Jesus with His disciples, we see intimate relationships modeled and extolled.

In Western culture we rarely value real, intimate closeness. In our very transient world, with quick discussions on the latest TV show or baseball game, we miss opportunities for closeness, sharing feelings with other important souls, people vital for our social, emotional, and spiritual growth.

The Trust of a Child

Shortly after I became a Christian, I met some young men who had a powerful and wonderful effect on my life. We met in high school and formed a rather mediocre musical group called "Children." As a group, we were as different as different can be. Jim Smith, a beautiful black brother who played bass and sang, is now a Baptist preacher in Texas. Andy Smith is a born-again Catholic who continues as a professional song writer in Nashville, Tennessee. Dr. Jerry Hom, who was our rhythm guitarist and back up singer, is a wonderful brother in God with a Chinese heritage and an amazing 4.0 grade point average, is now a cardiologist in San Francisco. Norman Johnson, who was our technical wizard and lead guitarist, is now a business executive. He played a "mean" guitar, and was our resident long-hair.

All of these men have gone on with their lives and have accomplished many good things.

My memories of them as a teenager are quite fond. You see, as we sang together, prayed together, and grew together, we developed a closeness and intimacy that provided a foundation for our emotional and spiritual growth.

Despite our problems, hang-ups and inconsistencies, and the many differences in our lives, we genuinely loved, and protected each other. In fact, the beauty of our relationship was that we knew enough about each other to get each other into trouble. Therefore, we had trust and confidence in each other's love.

We were and are brothers in Christ. The intimacy we had was powerful, and yet, incomplete. As times and circumstances have changed, so have our levels of commitment to each other.

Eventually, we all moved on in different directions, seeking to fulfill our lives in the Lord. How many of us long for that same level of intimate relationship; to have friendships where we can be just who we are without pretense, games or masks?

With my wife and children, I can be vulnerable. For most other people, it is a rare exception.

Jesus knows our need for deep relationship; it is imperative for our growth and development.

Our initial relationship with God begins an intimate fellowship with Him.

As with any relationship, deepening the fellowship takes time and effort. An intimate relationship with God is what enabled Jesus to understand completely His Father's will for His life, motivating him to do what God wanted Him to do.

The Scriptures note that Jesus was not surprised by anything that occurred because He knew the Father's heart. He could trust His Father's guidance no matter what He faced. Jesus reveals this in John 5:19 when He says,

"Verily, verily, I say unto you, The Son can do nothing of himself, but what he seeth the Father do: for what things soever he doeth, these also doeth the Son likewise." (KJV)

In their time of personal, intimate fellowship, God revealed His will to Jesus. We know that Jesus was given the Holy Spirit without measure and, consequently, operated in the gifts of the Spirit as each situation required.

In I Corinthians 12:7-12, Paul explains that God gives a manifestation of the Spirit to the Body by giving each person the gift of the Spirit. The Holy Spirit is the administrator of the gifts (manifestations) of the Spirit, and divides them as needed through whomever He chooses.

"But all these worketh that one and the selfsame Spirit, dividing to every man severally as he will. For as the body is one, and hath many members, and all the members of that one body, being many, are one body: so also is Christ" (I Corinthians 12:11-12).

When Christians, as members of the local Body, are in an intimate fellowship with God and with each other, God will reveal things in private and in the assemblies to help each person achieve purposes of God in that locality.

Together, Christians as a community make up Jesus' Body on this earth.

Therefore, the quality of fellowship with God determines how well Christians operate in the Spirit and power of God. When they spend their time with God, as is true with any relationship, they will learn His will and act according to that will.

Paraphrasing what J.R. Packer stated in his excellent book, *Knowing God,* there are three basic steps to begin the cultivation of a proper relationship with God. They are as follows:

1. Recognize and rejoice in God's unconditional love for you personally.
2. Consider God's character as revealed in His Word and work.

3. Read and listen to God's Word and strive to apply it to your own life.

Psychological research clearly shows that one of the primary needs of all human beings, regardless of their family background, is the need to feel loved and accepted by at least one other human being (we saw that earlier in our example of the Romanian orphans).

Our Lord understands this need in man better than anyone else, since it was our Creator who put that need in us from the moment of our creation.

> *"And the LORD God said, It is not good that the man should be alone; I will make him an help meet for him" (Genesis 2:18).*

God knows men and women have a need for love and acceptance. Often, people search for that sense of love and intimacy, as the country and western song says, "...in all the wrong places."

God has provided for Christians the ability to develop intimate, loving relationships with Him, and to assist them in making up for any deficiency in their lives through the relationship with Jesus Christ and with brothers and sisters in the Body of Christ.

America has recently experienced what was appropriately called the "ME generation." People seemed to be primarily interested only in what was good for them. In psychological terms, this is called "a state of narcissism," or self-absorption. This concept says, "I do not really care about what you need, I only care about what I need. I will use whatever or whomever it takes to meet my needs."

This entire concept of meeting personal needs by using others as objects is completely contrary to how Jesus taught and operated in His relationships. Jesus demonstrated an intimate lifestyle, modeled to those for whom He cared.

Though Jesus encountered a world filled with copious problems, He was completely comfortable with the disadvantaged and disenfranchised. He was not afraid to develop intimate relationships with people whom He knew would continually "fall short of the glory of God."

Through Jesus, God has shown us how much He desires intimate fellowship with each person. This same lifestyle, demonstrating true love, is a primary need of all mankind.

Everyone needs to know they are loved and accepted...just the way they are!

It is God's intention that all men be intimate in their relationships with Him and with each other. When close relationships are realized, a vital component in man's emotional, spiritual, and psychological needs is met. Jesus certainly knew the need for intimate relationship was imperative to growth and development. John says:

> *"In the beginning was the Word and the Word was with God, and the Word was God" (John 1:1).*

"Logos" is the Greek word "Word."

In the beginning was the logos, and the logos was with God, and the logos was God. Inherent in this is the reality that God the Father, God the Son, and God the Holy Spirit were in an intimate, unified relationship with one another. Unity in diversity is emulated in the Trinity; a picture of perfect intimacy.

> *"And the Word [logos, Who is Jesus] was made flesh, and dwelt among us, [or tabernacled with us] and we beheld his glory, the glory as of the only begotten of the Father, full of grace and truth" (John 1:14).*

That Word, the very mind and thought of God, the very person of God, became flesh to live amongst mankind, to have intimate fellowship with man here on earth.

How exciting it must have been for the disciples to have known Jesus in all of His fullness! John the apostle writes:

> *"That which was from the beginning, that which we have heard, that which we have seen with our eyes, which we have looked at and our hands have handled, this we proclaim concerning the Word of life. The Life appeared, we have seen*

*it and testify to it, and we proclaim to you the eternal life,
which was with the Father and has appeared to us. We
proclaim to you what we have seen and heard, so that you may
also have fellowship with us. And our fellowship is with the
Father and with his Son, Jesus Christ. We write this to make
our joy complete" (I John 1:1-4, NIV).*

The disciples must have had a significant sense of honor to have been with
Jesus, the Master. Jesus was the leader of this rag-tag group of disciples.
He called them, and dealt with them as family.

Jesus enjoyed His intimate communication with each of them. The Word
of God indicates He was touched by His disciples. He spent time with
them; He ate with them, drank with them, and modeled intimacy through
His vulnerability to them.

Jesus did not fear being touched by His friends, observed by His intimates.
In the 3 ½ years these men (and many women followers) spent with Jesus,
they observed his every mood, action and attitude. From His
compassionate responses to the weak and infirmed, to His supreme care
for children, to His disdain for the self-righteous, Jesus was real with His
friends, and demanded them to be real as well. His life was a challenge to
genuiness and righteousness, a challenge frequently failed by the
disciples, but without being made to feel the failure by Christ.

Modern Models of Jesus

It is unfortunate to observe models of leadership in the church that seem
so far from what Christ demonstrated and demands. Competition and
materialism abound. Professionalism appears more important than
realism. The hungry heart seeks close relationships with righteous
leaders, but can rarely get close enough to them to be impacted positively
for Christ.

Our example, our present-day Jesus, should be seen through the spiritual
leaders in the Body of Christ. We learn to walk according to the models
we observe. Just as children tend to model themselves after their parents,
so too, new Christians tend to model themselves after the leadership of the
local congregation. What we see in the leadership we will tend to become.
Jesus wanted His disciples to become just like Him, without apology.

When we come to know Christ as Savior, an intimate relationship begins. We become members of the family of God. The physical embodiment of the family of God is the local church.

As with a brand-new baby born into a home, an intimate relationship begins through bonding with the members of the Body of Christ.

In the natural, the initial bonding of a child is with Mom and Dad. That bond, we know, is forever. We use the term "blood is thicker than water" to indicate the depth of that bond.

Certainly, the same is to be true in the Body of Christ. The blood of Jesus unites us together in a bond that lasts forever.

It is important that we understand the bonding process, how it occurs, how intimate relationships are developed, and especially, how an intimate relationship with Christ is formed in a child of God.

Nurturing Through Love and Care

We all need to know love, closeness, and intimacy in our relationships. We need them naturally and spiritually.

A parent has an awesome responsibility in the raising and the nurturing of children. They must do all they can to ensure they grow strong and successful. Most parents understand this responsibility and discharge it well (though, of course not perfectly).

In the same way, spiritual fathers and mothers have the responsibility to provide an atmosphere conducive to growth, and to provide the proper training for new babes in Christ can grow in their relationship with the Lord.

Jesus was a perfect example of how to love and care. As a child, He experienced normal human development like the rest of humanity. He had His transition times where He began to discern His call for service.

Of most importance, the Word of God indicates He had an intimate relationship with His Father. Jesus speaks very clearly about His calling.

His dependency on God as His Father can be seen in His encounter with the spiritual leaders in Jerusalem (Luke 2:41-52) along with his understanding that His Father's business was His though it would be nurtured in his submitted relationship with His natural parents.

This dependency on God and others continued throughout His ministry, culminated in His upper room discourse and His willingness to submit to the cross. Jesus states in John 17:11,

> *"I will remain in the world no longer, but they are still in the world, and I am coming to you, Holy Father, protect them by the power of your name - the name you gave me so that they may be one, as we are one" (John 17:11, NIV).*

The most important hope for Jesus was that His disciples, His friends, would experience the quality of love he enjoyed with the Father that he enjoyed with them....and he wanted the same intimacy to be shared with disciples to follow.

Jesus was one with His Father.

We can have this intimacy with Christ, that sense of total love, because Jesus died for us, and we are in Him and He in us!

Not only did Jesus love us and desire intimacy with us, as He had with His Father, but He demonstrated a key ingredient to healthy relationships by subordinating His own needs to the needs of others.

> *"You heard me say, `I am going away and I am coming back to you.' If you loved me, you would be glad that I am going to the Father, for the Father is greater than I" (John 14:28, NIV).*

Jesus suffered and died and ascended into heaven, so the Holy Spirit could come and minister to others. Jesus subordinated His own needs for the needs of those He loved. (He even endured the pain of the cross.)

Jesus modeled His love to His disciples and, through His disciples, He continues to do so today in the Body of Christ. Our call is to develop the same quality of intimate relationship with Jesus Christ as His disciples did.

Paul's Example

Let us look at the life of Paul, as an example of how an intimate relationship is to be.

> *"That I may know Him, and the power of His resurrection and the fellowship of His sufferings, being conformed to His death"* *(Philippians 3:10, NAS).*

One of Paul's greatest desires was to be in total submission to the Lordship of Jesus Christ. To know Christ was the most important desire of Paul's life. The word "to know" used by Paul in this passage meant more than casual acquaintance, but meant to know him intimately, his thoughts, his heart, his desires, his ways. Paul's deepest desire, as he neared the end of his walk with Christ was to know him better.

That should be the quest of every new Christian, to know Christ, and desire to become mature and whole in God.

We seek to _know_ Him!

One of the condemning statements about the Church today is that we have lost our first love. Many who have been Christians for many years have lost that sense of deep relationship with God. As we walk in God, we must never lose the intimacy with the Lord, which is developed in the initial stages of our Christian walk. Our spiritual relationship with God is intended to grow, just as our relationship with our children, our wives, and our friends is to grow to maturity.

The First Step Toward This Relationship

How does this relationship develop?

What is the key to the development of this initial stage of spiritual growth?

To achieve this intimate relationship, we must be available and vulnerable to Jesus so He can encounter us and we can encounter Him by the Holy Spirit.

First, we must be available.

We must be willing as individuals to pray, to read God's Word, to be open to correction, vulnerable to the loving and caring probing of the Holy Spirit. We need to be willing to allow others to have input into our lives, and to share with us wisdom from their experience.

In the natural world, parents are to parent their children; children are never to parent their parents. One of the most problematic things seen in the counseling ministry is parents who are immature themselves and attempt to have their children meet their emotional needs. This immature approach cripples the child from being able to grow the way they should.

In the Body of Christ we need to have spiritual parents who are willing to be intimate and vulnerable with the spiritual children within the Church.

At the same time, spiritual children are not to say, "No, I do not want to have you as my parent." They need to be willing to submit themselves to this spiritual parenting process.

We must remember, as important as it is to develop relationships, human beings fear and avoid change. People can become stuck in their emotional or spiritual development, which hinders them from becoming whole people. It is easy to become comfortable in behavioral patterns; leading to negative habits which are resistant to change. This is a prime reason it is so hard to change a bad habit, be it overeating, or a critical spirit. We become comfortable in a pattern, and it is difficult to change.

Some may become continually self-absorbed with their unique problems. They become takers, and never givers. This can develop psychological/spiritual problems that are only too prevalent today, even in the Christian world.

God did not intend these problems to hinder His people. In truth, God's intention for all his children is to grow to maturity, to overcome various hindrances to our growth in God. The first step in overcoming and becoming is by developing a deep and abiding relationship with Christ. But we must remember, by Christ's own teaching, He alone (absent from all others) is not enough. He also wants us to become intimate with one another; to grow in all aspects of our lives.

"This is my commandment, That ye love one another, as I have loved you" (John 15:12).

We must be touchable!

Beyond becoming available and vulnerable, we must be willing to be touched, even as Jesus touched his disciples. Jesus was a touching person. He was not afraid to allow people to be close to Him, showing love and compassion. In John 13, Jesus washed the feet of His disciples.

> *"Then He poured water into the basin, and began to wash the disciples' feet and to wipe them with the towel with which He was girded." (John 13:5)*

When Simon Peter objected to this process, Jesus said, *"If I do not wash you, you have no part with Me." (John 13:8).*

To touch Peter's fee, he identified himself with his "walk," demonstrating a servant leader's heart to be willing to walk the road with others.

Jesus became a servant to all, and through His church He continues to serve as a demonstration of His love for all. Jesus cried, hurt, and modeled love and compassion to the world.

Psychologically touch is one of the most intimate forms of personal communication. Children, who are not touched, held and stroked, even though they may be fed, clothed and taken care of in physical areas, will suffer the pains of rejection, abandonment, and betrayal.

Children will die without proper love and care! This is also true in the spiritual realm.

Nothing is more painful to a pastor than to hear that a member of his or her congregation has been wounded, and that others who knew about it failed to help. When the hurting person is approached about coming back to church and to God, the stinging words the pastor most often hears are, "Where were you when I needed you?" In the world today there are thousands of "burnt stoves," formerly churched men and women who no longer darken a church door. Reasons for this can be myriad, but one that should never happen is a lack of care by God's people.

In order to touch and be touched, we must be vulnerable to each other. Vulnerability or openness and accessibility must flow from the mature to the young. A new Christian must be afforded the opportunity to feel safe, loved and cared for without judgment by those in leadership. This creates an atmosphere conducive to spiritual growth.

This atmosphere, as described by John and Peter include: grace and mercy, forgiveness and acceptance, inclusion and protection, all nurtured by the sincere milk of the Word. Now we turn to the ingredients for intimacy development and growth.

The Ingredients

Besides being available and vulnerable to God, there are several other primary ingredients that help to develop an intimate relationship with Christ and others.

First, as with natural children, to be able to grow and become strong in the natural world, safe environment must be developed to ensure proper and adequate care.

This environment is very similar to the planting of a garden. If you are expecting to grow a healthy crop which will produce fruit, you must have the right ingredients. The ground must be properly tilled, the weeds removed, the right nutrients sown, the proper seed planted, followed by plenty of water and sunshine for the seeds to grow. If you do not have the essential ingredients, you will not have a crop that will bear proper fruit.

Before you became a Christian, before you were born again, the garden of your life was under the ownership and operation of the devil. The devil sows into your life all kinds of foul ingredients that are destructive.

At the time of your conversion, the ownership of your property is turned over from Satan, and from your life, to the Lord Jesus Christ.

Although Jesus now owns the property, you must, with time, allow Him, by His Holy Spirit, to do the turning of the soil, the weeding, putting in the right ingredients, the preparation of the ground, the planting of the seed (which, of course, we know is the Word of God), knowing that with proper water and sunshine and care, fruit will be produced!

A healthy spiritual environment must be developed so we can grow strong in God.

The first component of that environment is unconditional love.

Dr. Carl Rogers used the term "unconditional positive regard," and in his terms, he meant we are to accept everything about the individual, even the bad things, and assume they are good. This level of acceptance goes beyond Scripture. The love of God is qualitatively different from humanistic acceptance.

When we come to know Christ as Savior, we learn that we are loved and accepted totally -- just the way we are. We are forgiven, we are accepted, we are included (1 John 2:12).

A good scripture to memorize to help you understand and apply love and acceptance is Philippians 4:8:

> *"Finally, brethren, whatsoever things are true, whatsoever things are honest, whatsoever things are just, whatsoever things are pure, whatsoever things are lovely, whatsoever things are of good report; if there be any virtue, and if there be any praise, think on these things."*

Recently, in a local church, one of the finest compliments received came from a woman who stated that when she and her family visited the church, they felt genuinely cared for and loved - just the way they were. They could not wait to return.

True love, demonstrated by affectionate, genuine acceptance is a primary ingredient of the environment that must be created for someone to grow in Christ.

People need to know they are loved and affirmed.

Trying New Things

The next stage of our human development is to move from self-centeredness or total dependence to independence. We do not grow and develop, move and change, unless we are allowed to try new things in our walk with God.

Our Christian potential is developed by learning to experience intimate fellowship in Christ. To do so, we need a biblical perception of who we are in God, and to develop an intimate bond with significant others in the local church.

Intimacy Is a Growth Process

Intimacy is developed -- through time and experience. It can be achieved by all of us, and it must be if we are to become all God wants us to be.

That is why your Christian fellowship is so vital. Make friends within the Body of Christ. Learn to trust and confide in them. Step by step, your relationship will grow into the nurturing, fulfilling intimacy God wants you to have.

Most psychologists look at the natural growth process through the life cycle as a series of stages of development all human beings must traverse.

Generally speaking, people process through these stages from birth to death in different ways and at different times. There is a general consensus that all must go through them for proper emotional development and health.

Similarly, there are some essential processes in developing intimate relationships in our spiritual walk. It is a process of growth that takes time and struggle, just as our physical development took time and struggle.

At birth, we are dependent upon our care-givers to provide us with everything we need -- food, clothing, shelter, the changing of diapers, burping, putting us to bed, getting us up in the morning, loving us, holding us.

Without care-givers, we could not survive.

As our children begin to grow, they master certain tasks essential for their emotional and physical survival. Though they may begin as sensing they are the center of the universe, with time, they learn to become a part of a family system.

They learn how to function and survive in the real world.

Though still quite dependent upon Mom and Dad, they continue to grow and mature, given the proper care, feeding, opportunity, and **positive encouragement!**

This is also true of our spiritual walk.

In reality, when we first come to know Jesus as our personal Savior, we are totally dependent upon Him. We are relatively helpless, since we do not know the spiritual principles God has provided for our protection.

Therefore, we cannot meet our own spiritual needs and, in most cases, we are unable to perform the basic rudimentary functions.

Once we are born again, although we are positionally complete in Christ, and in a right relationship with God, we must learn to grow, to become rooted deeper and deeper in Christ.

Despite our blood position in God's family, we realize that in our experience we struggle with many areas of life. The old nature, and things of sin, may continue to plague us.

Jesus said in John 16:33,

> *"These things I have spoken to you, so that in Me you may have peace. In the world you have tribulation, but take courage; I have overcome the world."*

Freedom in Christ

Secondly, there must be a certain percentage of freedom for people to be who they are. When a person first comes to know Christ, they often are rather rough around the edges. They do not know the right words to speak; they do not know how to find things in God; they do not know how to function and grow. They might wear jeans to church, have long, oily hair, and have more tattoos and body piercings than imaginable.

If we immediately place upon them rules that are stringent, regulations and requirements that immediately tell them they must change, we could stifle their growth.

We must allow for a certain amount of freedom for people to grow.

Given time, all new Christians, because they naturally desire to belong to this social group called "the Church," will learn how to behave in a manner more acceptable to the others in the congregation (and no doubt, the congregation will stretch!).

We must also provide a certain amount of freedom for people to make mistakes so we can **lovingly** correct them. Many Christians vastly misunderstand this important principle. If a new Christian brings her little boy to church (instead of putting him in the nursery), it is not loving to say, "Sister, I'm saying this in love -- your child makes far too much noise to be in this service" (the poor woman might not even know there is a nursery!).

Instead, you might say, "Sister, I know you are new to our church, so you might not know about the great nursery we have for handsome boys like your son. He'd probably enjoy himself a lot better in our toy-filled nursery than in the adult church service."

Our sensitivity to others provides for God's love to be expressed.

Discipline

Third, we must have appropriate **discipline**.

Discipline has four primary components to it.

The first component is of **clear expectations,** or structure. We must know how we are supposed to behave and function so we can be integrated into the group. Those expectations of how we are to live must be clearly stated, and validated by the Word of God.

Second, if we are going to give a clear expectation or structure, we must be willing to **supervise**, to shepherd the sheep -- we must be willing to follow up, to ensure the requirements we ask of people are actually being accomplished.

Third, we must have **consistent discipling** or **follow-through**. People must know we care enough to correct them when they are "not measuring up" in certain areas, or when they are not consistently following what is expected of them.

Finally, we must give encouragement, being able to see people through the eyes of faith, as better than they are. If we look at people as they were, with the sin of the past upon them, we may hinder their growth through a wrong attitude toward them.

When I first looked at my new-born child, I could not have said, "Please send her back, I can't deal with this mess." This precious child was my responsibility, no matter what the initial shock might have been. She was precious, beautiful, a gift from the Lord.

New Christians are not what they appear to be. They all will be transformed by the power of God! It is our responsibility to help nurture them through the transformation process. Encouragement to the people of God is a key to that process.

Let me illustrate this again from the natural world.

When we attempt to give a child a bath, we do not try to explain to a two-year-old the importance of cleanliness. They are not impressed by statements such as "Cleanliness is next to godliness."

What we do instead is give them a clear statement: "It is time to take your bath!"

Normally, when we give this instruction, we do not sit in our armchair and expect the child to go upstairs, get undressed, draw the water, climb into the tub, scrub clean, get out, and dry off.

As parents, we know we must supervise the bathing process! That is why the parent takes the child by the hand and leads them into the bathroom to be bathed. The consistent follow-through comes when we participate with them and show them how to put the soap on the cloth and apply it to the areas of their body that need to be cleaned.

Finally, when they are all cleaned, pressed, and dried, we usually encourage them by saying something like: "Doesn't it feel wonderful to be clean? You smell so good."

The process with new babes in Christ is not materially different. These new "children" need to be taken by the hand, told how to live, how to read, how to study, how to become God's person. We need to consistently supervise and follow through with them; they need encouragement to grow in God.

The Fundamentals

There are a few basic, fundamental truths each believer must learn. Many of these fundamental spiritual elements are found in my book, *New Beginnings: A Sure Foundation*. These fundamental spiritual elements are outlined here, but the reader, especially the new Christian, is recommended to read and to study *New Beginnings: A Sure Foundation*. It will help your growth in Christ.

Just as in the military, where basic training is needed to train individuals to become soldiers, people have to be trained to become intimate in God, and soldiers for the King of kings.

Spiritual Training

Here are the requirements to become a soldier for Jesus:

1. We must experience true forgiveness of our sins.

In I John 2:12-13c, the apostle with whom Jesus had the most close and intimate relationship describes the first stage of spiritual development: the stage of the little child.

"I write unto you, little children, because your sins are forgiven you for his name's sake...I write unto you, little children, because ye have known the Father."

As a child, it is imperative that the new Christian know that his/her sins are fully forgiven, and that he/she knows "Abba," Daddy, Father. Forgiveness of all sins from the past, present and future is a most liberating concept, to be rejoiced in each day of our life. When we know we are forgiven, we know we belong in the family. We are forgiven because of the Father's great love; our Papa is the greatest Papa of all. Further, intimacy with Daddy/Father must be learned through the simple disciplines to follow.

2. We must learn to pray.

Prayer is nothing more than communicating with God. Most new Christians do not know how to pray! In most cases, we need to start people where they are: allow them to use their own language structure to communicate with God.

Pontifical pious prayers with powerful professions of passion will not happen in the beginning stages. Children start with simple sounds, and simple prayer (Be merciful unto me a sinner!) can be most profound. In prayer, we can demonstrate true intimacy with a new convert. We are personal, practical, and passionate in our prayers with a new believer, we model for them intimacy which is caught more than taught. We must remember early patterns tend to be lasting ones. Rigid, religious prayers will make future intimacy in prayer with our loving Father more difficult.

Prayer is of vital importance. Especially in difficult times, prayer and prayer warriors are necessary to move the Church forward. We need to teach people how to pray, how to do so properly, and the reality that God hears and answers our prayers.

Jesus spent a significant amount of time in prayer. He was in constant communication with His Father. He rose early; He stole away and made prayer time a priority.

We do not necessarily need to get up early in the morning to be in communion with God. I happen to pray better after my mind is cleared of the cobwebs, but it is, nonetheless, essential that prayer become an important discipline of life.

Initially, how do new babes in Christ learn to pray? They learn by praying with more seasoned Christians, and by following their pattern. It is because of this that we need good role models for young Christians within the Body of Christ.

3. We must learn how to study God's Word.

Most Christians have not read the entire Word of God (even Christians who have been saved for many years). Most of us read some of it, but usually, in sporadic fashion. We must learn and teach new babes in Christ how to study God's Word in a systematic way, not haphazardly.

New Christians need to learn, becoming discipled to understand the important themes of the Word of God. Very simply, the Bible is God's communication of love to each of us. It is important for a new Christian to start reading in the book of John (especially John 3), then move on to the book of I John. It is in the gospel of John, and in the epistles of John, that we best see the intimate relationship with God through His Son, Jesus Christ demonstrated.

Remember, John was called the "beloved one." He was the one most intimate with Christ.

It is through the reading of the Word that we understand the heart of God. When John wrote, he shared from his heart. It is important we learn what great love the Father has for us. One caution must be observed. Most assume everyone reads, and reads well. We further assume when new Christians are told to read the gospel, that they actually do so.

In reality, many Christians never do complete the reading of the gospel of John. We fail to follow up and ensure it is read adequately.

The study of God's Word must be done on a regular, systematic basis. To go even a day without reading His Word means we are not eating a full diet of what will help us grow. A day without food would leave us weak; two or three days without food and we would not be able to defend ourselves.

So too with God's spiritual food.

Each day away from the bread of life leaves us weaker and weaker, until finally we are unable to resist even the most minimal attacks of the enemy.

Very few of us would go without a meal in any given day except for times of fasting. We should never go without the Word of God in our lives. For more information on this subject, read *Fresh Manna: How to Study God's Word*.

4. Christians Need Fellowship.

There is a strong need for fellowship within the Body of Christ. Fellowship means to have quality time with other Christians. It does not necessarily mean we have to sit down and read the Bible together, or have a pot-luck, although fellowship does occur during these times.

Fellowship means being together, talking together, sharing our lives with one another. The central focus of sharing is the Lord.

This is what Jesus did with His disciples. Jesus taught His disciples how to minister one to another. He ate with them and walked with them. Jesus taught them by His behavior, by His words, by illuminating the Word of God to them through His ministry and teaching. He imparted Himself to His disciples. Jesus even encouraged their neediness and questions.

Oh, how I wish, as parents, we could grasp the privilege we have to hear the questions of our children!

I wish pastors and spiritual leaders could understand that the questions of new babes in Christ are important, and vital to their spiritual growth!

We need to answer all questions to the best of our ability. The willingness to be with our new converts is essential. We need to include them in our activities so they can see what it means to really live the Christian life. To do this, we must walk in an intimate relationship with Jesus ourselves, and be vulnerable to our "sheep." This is an essential element of real fellowship.

5. We need to learn how to praise and worship.

All people worship. It is important for a new Christian to understand "why" we should praise and worship our Lord.

A dear friend and a brother in the Lord, Dr. Michael Elliot, shares with great clarity the reason why we need to praise and worship. In his wonderful book called *Redemption the Foundation of Worship* he presents the primary premise of worship. According to Dr. Elliot, the angels were originally created to bring praise and worship to God. Lucifer was the leader of heaven's praises! When Lucifer led the rebellion against God, there was a need to have others who would bring praise and worship to God. He created mankind for this purpose, and for fellowship with Himself.

The Word of God says God inhabits the praises of His people (Psalm 22:3). He hears our praise, and in that place of praise, God inhabits us or infiltrates our very lives. It blesses the Lord and it blesses us when we give praise and worship to the Lord.

> *"Shout joyfully to the LORD, all the earth. Serve the LORD with gladness; Come before Him with joyful singing."* (Psalm 100:1-2)

We have seen forms of apostasy develop throughout Church history. Historically, many of the basic biblical doctrines were lost or set aside for a season. God is now restoring all of these back to the Church, line upon line, precept upon precept.

One of the primary teachings restored to the church is the vital importance of the praise and worship of our Father God.

Worship of the Lord is a primary ministry to the Lord. We worship Him through singing, through praise, through spiritual gifts, and most importantly, through obedience. We must be true worshipers in Spirit and in truth through the exhibition of the fruit of the Holy Spirit in our lives. Part of that fruit is a life of personal praise.

How do people learn to praise and worship?

The same way they learn to pray. By watching and hearing praise and worship within the local church. New creations observe praise, see it modeled in the leadership within the Body of Christ. If leaders are not praisers and worshipers, if they do not make it a priority, babes in Christ will learn to downplay its importance, in spite of our vociferous exhortations.

Today we need to do things together as a spiritual family. Corporate worship is designed to remove barriers between us, and mold us as the family of God. In worshipping God, we learn to minister to Him, and learn to minister to one another.

6. We need to witness.

One of the most fundamental needs within the Church today is for active witnesses. New converts need to learn to share their faith in an intimate and effective manner.

This is one of the first things we teach in our discipleship training program. It is at the very beginning of our new walk that we have the greatest influence for Christ with people in our sphere of family and friends.

We must systematically teach new converts how to share their faith. Sharing the Lord with others is one of the ways to grow in God. I have discovered that if one can give their testimony within 48 hours after coming to know Christ, they will learn to become an effective witness for the rest of their lives.

I Remember

When I was first saved, I was asked to turn around and face the congregation, and, in my own simple way, tell them what Jesus had done in my life. All I could remember was that I now had a friend in Jesus, and I felt clean and whole. I have never ceased to share that Jesus still does the same for people today. Witnessing is a key part of our spiritual growth; we must encourage new converts to break the fear of sharing their faith, and learn the joy of sharing life with others.

7. All believers must be baptized in water and in the Holy Spirit.

New believers need water baptism, signifying their symbolic death and resurrection with Christ.

Further, they need to be immersed in the Holy Spirit so they have the power of God to be witnesses and to live a holy life. Without the power of the Holy Spirit, they never become what God intends them to be.

8. We need family.

The need for family in Western culture is incredible! We could learn much from our "Two thirds world brothers," where tribe and family is so meaningful.

We call ourselves, and the Word of God states we are, "the family of God." Therefore, it follows it is important to know what it takes to have a healthy and whole family. There are five primary characteristics of a healthy, natural family, which can also be mirrored in the family of God.

a. Every family needs to have a sense of consistency and predictability.

New babes in Christ are coming out of a chaotic world. In Ephesians 2, Paul states we were, by nature, "*children of wrath.*" We were totally dead in our trespasses and sins, without hope, groping about in a chaotic world of darkness, attempting to find security and significance.

New Christians need consistency and predictability, especially in the church. This is to be modeled in our local congregation. Thus, our traditions, if meaningfully taught, provide an important foundation for growth.

There is a valid need for structure in the home and in the church, so people feel safe. Too many changes - the constant moving of staff and programs - set the stage for fear and lack of confidence in the leadership, which threatens security. We need stability and predictability, structure and order, through which the Spirit of God can move. We live our lives according to patterns, and good patterns can carry us throughout our lifetime.

b. New family members must have freedom to express their emotions and feelings with acceptance and understanding.

The natural family needs this, and so does God's spiritual family. We need not squelch people because of their individuality, but we must teach them how to say and do God's will as expressed through His Word.

c. A healthy family must have constructive relationships.

New Christians must understand the importance of fitting into the family, as a functioning member. People have a need to belong. We need to provide that sense of belonging in the Body of Christ. Church leadership must emphasize the Body concept, not playing favorites because of personality, gender, or race. We all have a placement in the Body of Christ. Leadership must assist the new convert to find his/her place in Christ.

d. There needs to be an ability to share common goals, and yet allow for individual differences.

The Word of God says that *"Where there is no vision, the people perish"* (Proverb 29:18). And, we perish for *"lack of knowledge"* (Hosea 4:6).

We need to have common goals to know we fit in, becoming a part of something greater than ourselves. This happens in the natural growth process through the developmental stages of a child, and it should occur within the Church.

If we properly train and teach our people the goals and vision for the local congregation, we will assist them in finding a place of service. Allowing for the gifts and callings of individuals in the body makes room for them to begin bearing fruit that will endure.

e. In a healthy family, there must be an ability to subordinate personal needs for group needs.

Everyone has a place, and all have a function. It is inherent within the leadership of the local church to demonstrate the ability to lay aside personal needs for the needs of the group. The Church should emulate the motto, "Sowing our lives for something greater than ourselves."

Final Thoughts in Intimacy

We need to develop our relationship with Jesus Christ and with others to grow to the full measure of the man and woman of God we are to become. This occurs as we learn the basics, become vulnerable with one another, and through modeling intimacy within relationships. Obedience to God's Word and submission to legitimate authority will produce healthy growth in the family of God.

Christ humbled Himself and became submissive to the Father, and it is important for the children of God to learn to do the same.

> *"And being found in fashion as a man, he humbled himself, and became obedient unto death, even the death of the cross"(Philippians 2:8).*

Christ emptied Himself of His divine nature. (Dr. Ken Chant, in his book *Christian Life*, describes this process in great depth.) This is the beginning - but God wants us to continue our journey beyond security, never leaving the intimate relationship, while recognizing our need to conform to Christ's image.

New Christians who have come out of darkness into God's marvelous light, find a place to belong. That is a therapeutic stage, but it is not therapy. We must go beyond our initial stage of childhood into the HEALING COMMUNITY.

We must enter the wilderness experience of the "healing community," where the character flaws inflicted upon us by the world are removed by God's grace and mercy.

In God's "Healing Community" growth and maturity in Christ are an ongoing process, not just an event. This necessary, God-given process will be discussed next.

Questions for Discussion and Meditation

1. How do we know a young Christian is ready for the next step? How can we be sure not to push her or him too fast in their spiritual growth process?

2. What exactly is a full measure of a man or woman in this relationship with God? What might cause a believer to stop growing in Christ?

3. How can we best allow the Lord to work in our lives and be totally submitted to Him?

4. Relate to one other person your experience in the first few weeks/months of your spiritual walk. What would you change about your experience?

5. If you were to lead someone to Christ, how would you disciple them?

SECTION TWO

THE HEALING COMMUNITY

Young Men

I have written to you, young men, because you are strong, and the word of God abides in you, and you have overcome the evil one."

1 John 2:12-14

CHAPTER SIX

THE TRANSFORMATION
OF CHARACTER

Back to my own story.

After I was first saved, I continued to grow in God for a period of time because of the natural, compulsive part of my nature. I had waited from the age of twelve until I was almost eighteen before I experienced the full infilling of the Holy Spirit. This was a necessary step of faith on my part. Around age sixteen, although I knew I had a call of God on my life, I began to recognize a dryness and an emptiness in my spirit.

I had the Christian basics down: I would read the word, pray, fellowship, and witness. I was doing all of the right things, and yet, I had no real sense of power, no sense of purpose, and was struggling with some very significant problem areas in my life.

I knew I needed something more from God, but I did not know specifically what that was, or how to get it.

I remember discussing my emptiness with my pastor, and he advised that all I could do was to pray, fellowship, and witness, because essentially, that is all there was for me in God.

Well, after my discussion with my pastor, I increased my prayer time, seeking God with all of my heart. As I did, the Lord began to reveal to me Scriptures about the infilling of the Holy Spirit. I began to diligently seek after this experience. I remember attending a church God told me to visit, knowing that I would receive the infilling of the Holy Spirit. I went, I experienced a marvelous outpouring of God's Spirit on my life, and the results were significant.

Of course, being a naive young man, I expected my entire life would now change. I expected to come away from this experience and never again have problems to face.

That certainly was not the case.

When I was filled with the Holy Spirit, I returned to my young people's group at the little church in which I was raised. I shared with them this marvelous experience of having been filled with the Holy Spirit; I knew many of them shared similar feelings of frustration of not having the power to walk a deeper walk with God.

Well, the results of my sharing were not what I expected. In fact, I was told that if I did not renounce this new experience (which was probably "of the devil"), I would no longer fit into the family of God; there would no longer be a place for me in my local church.

I was asked to leave, and told never to return.

This was a terribly difficult time in my life, and yet, I knew my experience was real and truly from God. I had not done anything other than what the Bible said to do. Yet, because I did not fit into the belief system of that local assembly, I was excluded from my church family, a family that had become very important to me.

In some ways, this experience is a sad commentary on church life, and yet, the Lord never forsook me. I soon found wonderful fellowship under Dr. Joseph Bohac, my new mentor, and I began to move on in the things of God.

Let me point out something very specific here.

At the moment I was filled with the Holy Spirit, I received a renewal of power and zest in my life. Of course, the Holy Spirit was already in my spirit, or I could not be born again. My hunger for "more" led me to a deeper infilling, opening the gifts of the Holy Spirit to me, along with a passion and power for witness. But it did not solve my characteristic deficiencies (anger, fear, etc.) I still had many problem areas from my old nature. The infilling of the Holy Spirit was not a magic pill that ended all of my problems; yet it was another step toward becoming what God wanted me to be, of yielding my life to the Lordship of Jesus Christ.

One thing I have discovered through the years is there is no such thing as the "final step" towards being a mature Christian or a mature church. We are always in a progression of steps, hopefully heading for a "Christ-like" lifestyle. There is no such thing as a totally mature community, and there is no such thing as a totally mature person.

Conditions exist, however, which make the steps toward maturation easier. Presented here is an outline of the essential characteristics of a community able to assist people in maturing in their walk with God. Remember, the Lord desires for us to grow in Him. The Apostle John, understanding this developmental process, writes:

"I am writing to you, young men, because you have overcome the evil one...I have written to you, young men, because you are strong, and the word of God abides in you, and you have overcome the evil one" (1 John 2:13b, 14b)

To achieve the overcomer's crown, there had to be things to overcome, lessons to be learned. Similar to the children of Israel in the wilderness, who had to become obedient to God and learn dependency on Him, we must overcome the ravages of old, "Egyptian" lifestyles. This happens through spiritual warfare. Ephesians 6:10-18 states:

"Finally, be strong in the Lord and in the strength of His might. Put on the full armor of God, so that you will be able to stand firm against the schemes of the devil. For our struggle is not against flesh and blood, but against the rulers, against the powers, against the world forces of this darkness, against the spiritual forces of wickedness in the heavenly places. Therefore, take up the full armor of God, so that you will be able to resist in the evil day, and having done everything, to stand firm. Stand firm therefore, having girded your loins with truth, and having put on the breastplate of righteousness, and having shod your feet with the preparation of the gospel of peace; in addition to all, taking up the shield of faith with which you will be able to extinguish all the flaming arrows of the evil one. And take the helmet of salvation, and the sword of the Spirit, which is the word of God. With all prayer and petition pray at all times in the Spirit, and with this in view, be on the alert with all perseverance and petition for all the saints." (NAS)

Through our warfare, as we abide in the vine (John 15), through abiding in God's Word, we become strong. This process, the process of becoming an overcomer, is what the healing community is all about. All healing from the damage done by inherited and committed sin prior to knowing Christ must be confronted and transformed. This begins and ends with our relationship with the Lord. Therefore, we start again with the Intimate Relationship.

1. **There must be an intimate relationship developed with our Lord and with one another.**

Remember, intimacy must be nurtured in a community structure that allows us to grow, develop, and learn what acceptance truly is.

In the very beginning of all things, Jesus as the Word was in complete unity with the Father and the Holy Spirit. There was oneness, a totality (John 1:1).

When Jesus came to the earth, He did so to bring reconciliation back to humanity. God's plan was to bring people to salvation, to wholeness and completeness.

Of course, we must realize the difference between where someone is and where God intends them to be. If you do not know the plan God has for an individual's life, then you cannot help fulfill that plan as a care-giver.

God wants to meet the deep, underlying, intimate needs of people through relationship in the Body. When Jesus ministered, He accepted people right where they were, and so must we.

As previously stated, in the natural world, when a child is born, it is totally dependent upon care-givers. A bond develops, and a sense of trust is created as needs are met.

New Christians are much like a brand-new child, entering the church with hurts, misconceptions, and hungry souls needing nourishment and care. They are alive in God, but they still have many things they need to work through to live healthy fulfilling lives.

The foundation of intimacy with Christ and his body, as demonstrated in Jesus' discipleship model is the first and most impatient stage of our maturing process. (1 John 1:1-5).

You can see how vital intimacy was to the apostles. There must be intimacy and warmth developed in our relationships, just as Christ developed warmth and intimacy with the apostles. The keys to intimacy include:

a. **Unconditional love**, without condemnation - accepting a person just as they are and loving them as a creature of God.

b. **Freedom to express** who they are - even if they are not like us. Jesus opened the doors to a huge variety of individuals to enter the Kingdom of God. We all want to fit into a social group, and so the new Christian will eventually conform to the church in which they choose to worship.

c. **Discipline** is a part of discipleship. Give loving help while establishing boundaries for the new Christian through the Word of God, and through wisdom and common sense. Again, these are the first steps.

2. Children must continue to grow and change.

What a tragedy it would be if a child at age eighteen was still running around in diapers. I do not think any of us would want this to happen to our child.

Neither should brand-new babes in Christ just drink the milk of the Word; they need to learn to grow and become whole and complete in God, to eat the transforming and empowering meat of God's Word (Hebrews 5:12,14).

In my own life, there were areas I knew had to change. Though I was active in church, able to witness and outwardly had it "together" like most (all really), I carried attitudes, beliefs, and wounds from the past that needed change. Of course, I had to be willing to submit to the process of change. But how? What was the process for change? Was there a biblical prescription and examples that were sound biblically and wise psychologically to change?

My search for the answers to these questions was both personal and professional. By age 18-20, I had been in church for several years. During my young life, I knew of many believers who struggled incessantly with besetting sins. Honest saints struggled with issues of sin and weight of care, with limited relief being offered. My own life was often less than pleasing to God (or to myself or to my friends for that matter). I believed in victory, had heard victory was ours, but rarely saw living testimony of Christ's victorious life in them (or myself). My heart broke (and still breaks) over this needless condition that limits believers from fulfilling God's destiny. This led me to the search of the principles of change developed here.

3. It is vital to be a part of a healing community.

God desires us to mature beyond the basics of our Christian walk, to experience the "healing community." God desires us to become full, functional, mature, equipped.

Leaders must develop a vision for equipping young Christians, bringing them to maturity, leading them into a caring and healing community called the Church.

All believers need identification with the family of God, willing to minister to people who have hurts and needs. People may know the basic rules of right and wrong, they may know what is acceptable and unacceptable within the family of God.

But, that is not enough!

They need to know how to appropriate the principles of God's Word, applying them effectively to real life. This process will help ensure that their vital needs will be met.

After we come to know Christ and begin to grow in the basic areas of Christian life; as we read and understand God's Word, pray effectively, praise God, and worship Him in Spirit and in truth, we develop functionality within the family of God. We can become comfortable for a season. This is not only allowed, but necessary for our protection. But a day comes, as natural as the terrible twos, when we, led by the Holy Spirit, begin to hunger for more, and become vulnerable to enemy attack. Even this is necessary to our growth in Christ, as necessary as allowing a child to explore their world.

The Holy Spirit will speak to us about areas of our lives that will need to change and mature.

As we begin to grow in God, the Holy Spirit will quicken our hearts, and touch our minds to reveal areas of our characters which are not in compliance with the Lord's will. As He does so, it will become necessary for us to begin to proceed through a process of change and growth that is a life-long challenge. This is natural and God-directed.

The mind is the place where changes take place. The mind is the analyzing, evaluating, critical thinking part of man. The struggle to dominate and control the mind is the struggle to dominate man himself. Even the battle between God and Satan takes place in the battleground of our mind. God's goal is that we inherit His promises and become an overcomer in the Kingdom; to overcome means battle!

Thoughts Determine Behavior
Some Cautions During Your Wilderness Walk

The process of change has been best documented in the natural world through research in the field of "cognitive psychology." In this discipline, researchers have developed three primary keys, or components of change, which are appropriate to Christians as they progress in their walk with God - becoming transformed to the image of Christ. These three components are:

1. Change of environment: The first step to change is to start something or stop something.

When we stop doing whatever we are normally doing, and try to change, that change is usually temporary - unless the underlying core problem is resolved. We see this all the time in people who go on diets. If they fail to deal with root causes, they will gain weight again just as soon as the diet is over.

2. Change in thinking or belief systems:

This is the hardest part. To change one's thinking takes time. New information must be gained, new, learned principles applied. From a biblical point of view the heart must be transformed through the Word.

3. Practice, practice, practice:

Practice makes perfect, if you practice healthy principles. Once right principles are known, they must be operationalized in the real world. From a biblical view, we must "faith it" until we "make it." You operate in faith believing God will transform you into the person you want to be, and you begin thanking Him for what you will be - even before you reach that goal. In the process of positive affirmation, coupled with the action of "acting" friendly, or whatever change you desire, you will find your thinking process and core beliefs starting to change.

Some Hindrances

All of our lives we have been told who we are by society, by our parents, by our educational system, and the resulting image of ourselves may have hurt us. Any message you hear often enough becomes a learned "I am." These "I am" messages, many of which are not true, can cause distortions in how life is perceived and lived.

Messages such as "I am no good," "I am a bum," "I am a poor student," "I am hopeless," "I am clumsy," "I am too fat," and hundreds of others seem to forever ring within our minds.

On the other side of the spectrum, there are those who fight perfectionism – "I ought" to be slimmer, smarter, holier, etc. Be careful. These thoughts can lead to bondage and legalism. We must try to remove the "oughts" from our vocabulary.

One of the things Jesus wants for us, as He renews our minds, is to help us know who we are in Him. We need to understand we are the righteousness of God in Christ. This is one of the many new "I am" messages that are given to us in the Word of God.

The new Christian can be taught to learn new "I am's." "I am a child of the King," "I can do all things through Christ," "I am a victor and not a victim," "I am strong through the Holy Spirit Who lives within me," and a hundred more "I am" messages can be learned through scripture and discipleship.

We have talked about the process of putting off the old, renewing our mind, and putting on the new (Ephesians 4:17-32).

In Ephesians 5:1-2, we see the need to imitate Christ and become just like Him.

> *"Be ye therefore followers of God, as dear children; And walk in love, as Christ also hath loved us, and hath given himself for us an offering and a sacrifice to God for a sweet-smelling savour."*

The third component to ultimately changing our lives on a permanent basis is practice, practice, practice!

After we have changed the way we see the world, or have repented (which means changing our thinking about something from a worldly view to a biblical and Christian view), we must then practice new behavior and attitudes, learning to walk in righteousness.

These components of change are all necessary, as you will see as we go through this process of the healing community.

It is important to note that except for our position in Christ, which is instantaneously acquired at the time of our salvation, **ALL CHANGE, especially in our character or personality is usually a process that takes time!**

I have found it takes approximately forty days of performing a new behavior and avoiding an old one for the desired behavior to become a new habit.

This is why many people never seem to make the changes necessary to change their lives. They become discouraged and quit before a permanent change can take place. This also indicates why we need to encourage one another in the Body of Christ toward good works and devotion to Christ.

There are many children who seem to have the ability to be loving, kind, and gentle by nature. There are others who seem to be very strong-willed, and inherently want to "do their own thing." They act contrary to the rules and goals of the family. These children are definitely more challenging. Yet, in most cases, a mother or father would abhor the suggestion of sending them out of their home because they were not as compliant as another child.

At times, if a child needs a special environment, separation from the natural home might be necessary. Certainly there are cases where this is necessary, but a special environment is always a last resort.

The goal of the family is to raise and train the child to a place where they are mature enough to be out on their own. We want our children to be functioning members of society, in the family system, and in the world at large.

The Elements of Change Expanded

If we are going to change anything, such as an unwanted eating behavior, **we must first change our environment**. That could be the internal or external behaviors and attitudes of the individual.

For instance, for someone to lose weight, it would be necessary for them to eat less. That is a change in environment. But for a true change to occur, there must be more than a change in behavior. If one only changes behavior externally (as many have done countless times), they will put the weight right back on.

Even after they have successfully changed the environment for a period of time, permanent results may not be seen. Ultimately, therefore, there must be **a change in belief or perception**. A person must be able, using the analogy of weight loss, to see themselves as thin and attractive, and deserving of health and fitness.

Only the change in perception will allow permanent change to occur.

The "flesh" that Christians so often speak about is really the world within - the sum total of our desires and appetites, needs and drives that strive for self-gratification. After the fall of man, "the flesh" became the principal component of "sin" in man.

> *"Each one is tempted and he is carried away and enticed by his own lust" (James 1:14 - 15).*

Information from the environment is relayed to the mind through the senses: touch, smell, hearing, etc. It is important for us, as Christians, to develop a discerning process and a critical attitude toward what we see, hear, touch, feel, smell - so we are not constantly exposed to the pressures and influences of the world.

The second component of change is an alteration in the **internal thinking and perception**. We must be able to perceive ourselves (in the Spirit) as children of God, created in His image, and think (in our mind) the good things of God, to eventuate change.

Any real change always involves far more than altering our sinful behavior patterns - it involves allowing the Spirit of God to renew us - to change our essential thoughts. A renewed mind includes the healing of hurts and past traumas, becoming whole in Jesus Christ.

To experience the mind-renewal process, the following steps are suggested:

1. Pray for the Holy Spirit to guide you and change your self-talk.

Remember, *"As a man thinketh in his heart, so is he" (Proverbs 23:7).* As you pray, ask the Holy Spirit to help you do the following:

   a. Locate those areas of thought that are "misbeliefs" - thoughts that are harming you in some way.
   b. Once the Holy Spirit has helped isolate these "negative" thoughts, ask Him to help change the thoughts to more "positive" and productive patterns.
   c. Ask the Holy Spirit to help you think only those thoughts that are true and in line with God's will and heart.

2. Search for scriptural principles to guide you.

"Holiness" comes from the Hebrew and Greek words which mean "to set apart or separate for sacred purposes; to consecrate; pronounce clean."

Isn't that wonderful?

You are in a process of being washed, cleansed, and made "spotless" to the glory of God!

"Follow peace with all men, and holiness, without which no man shall see the Lord" (Hebrews 12:14).

Remember, your process of becoming holy and walking in sanctification comes only through the love and power of Jesus Christ. For some, the process is almost instantaneous with their salvation. For most, the process takes time.

As we mature God in, we must not sit around waiting to become holy. There is always the danger of becoming so "inward" in thinking, so determined to become "more mature and more holy" before serving God in ministry, the actual ministry never takes place.

3. Meditate on these spiritual principles. Not just memorize Scripture, but think about that Scripture and ask the Holy Spirit to make it part of life.

> *"Oh, how I love your law! It is my meditation all the day....Your word is a lamp to my feet and a light to my path."* (Psalm 119:97, 105)

> *"But his delight is in the law of the LORD; and in His law he meditates day and night. He will be like a tree firmly planted by streams of water, which yields its fruit in its season and its leaf does not wither; and in whatever he does, he prospers."* (Psalm 1:2-3)

As you meditate on these Scriptures, remember:

a. Have the **FAITH** to believe God wants to speak to us about the details of our life. Through His Holy Spirit, He will reveal spiritual truths and breakthroughs to us.
b. **OBEY** those things the Holy Spirit prompts you to do.
c. **ASK** God to touch and heal those areas that need to be transformed. This will almost always involve forgiving others who have hurt you.

Freedom, Not Bondage

Remember, Jesus came to set you free from rebellion, bondage, guilt and shame!

As we move toward the end of this section, I would like to comment on specific portions of Scripture which I believe will help you in catching the vision of what the *Journey to Wholeness* means.

In Matthew 25, verses 35-40, we read the following:

> *"For I was hungry, and you gave me something to eat; I was thirsty, and you gave me something to drink; I was a stranger, and you invited me in; naked, and you clothed me; I was sick, and you visited me; I was in prison, and you came to me. Then the righteous will answer Him, saying, Lord, when did we see you hungry, and feed you, or thirsty, and give you something to drink? And when did we see you a stranger, and invite you in, or naked, and clothe you? When did we see you sick, or in prison, and come to you? The King will answer and say to them, "Truly I say to you, to the extent that you did it to one of these brothers of mine, even the least of them, you did it to me."* (Matthew 25:35-40)

As Christians, we all desire, to fit into the family of God. The Bible tells us that each of us has a functional place within the Church, we have a purpose in God.

Unfortunately, many were made to feel as if we were not important in our birth families. Some were scapegoats, some labeled the "good ones" and some the "bad ones." Many of us have had difficult experiences within our family of origin as we tried to grow and mature as human beings.

Unfortunately, the same process can occur in church.

God intended the family of God to be a nurturing, caring, healing community of fellow strugglers. These fellow strugglers, as God created them to be, need to achieve success in the things of God. Local churches are urged to develop a healing place where relationships can grow in God, and in one another, where true healing, character change, and transformation of the inner man will be possible, and where compassion for the world will be evident.

The outgrowth of this nurturing will be a life that is committed to seeing others won to Jesus Christ.

Remember, the *Journey to Wholeness* is a process; it evolves. It is important to remember:

1. Change takes time. Of course, God can change you miraculously in an instant, but for most of us, it is an on-going process.

2. Your emotions and actions will sometimes "lapse" into old patterns. Do not despair. That is part of the transformation process.

When you lapse into old beliefs, it is important to identify them as being from the "old man."

> *"We are not ignorant of his (Satan's) thoughts" (II Corinthians 2:11).*

I would even suggest you ask God to show you your old beliefs - for the purpose of confronting these false concepts. David's prayer can help:

> *"Search me, O God, and know my heart: try me, and know my thoughts: And see if there be any wicked way in me, and lead me in the way everlasting"* (Psalm 139:23-24).

Once you have acknowledged the "old man" left in you, get it out of your life!

> *"But now you also, put them all aside: anger, wrath, malice, slander, and abusive speech from your mouth." (Colossians 3:8)*

Appropriate the cross[1] and ask God to destroy the "old man" fragments left in you once and for all!

> *"For if you are living according to the flesh, you must die; but if by the Spirit you are putting to death the deeds of the body, you will live. For all who are being led by the Spirit of God, these are sons of God. For you have not received a spirit of slavery leading to fear again, but you have received a spirit of*

---

[1] Meaning, accept the fact that Christ finished the work of redemption for you on the cross. You died with Him. You live with Him!

adoption as sons, by which we cry out, "Abba! Father!"
Romans 8:13-15

3. Keep your expectations reasonable. Do not expect too much too fast. Change is a process. Each time you experience new beliefs - beliefs in line with God's Word and will for your life - Acknowledge the growth and thank God for His grace to change. Just as David did, cry out to the Lord:

> *"Create in me a clean heart, O God, And renew a steadfast spirit within me"* (Psalm 51:10).

4. Do not pretend that you are changing if you are not! Stay honest with yourself, stay open to the Holy Spirit, and your transformation will take place!

With each change, proclaim the new person you are in Christ, and praise God for it!

As you grow, you will learn to recognize those parts of the transformed you that are fitting and proper, aligned the way God intended. Some general rules you can apply to test your growth and make certain you are headed in the right direction are as follows:

1. Your growth must be in accordance and compliance with Scripture.

2. Your growth should be realistic, and take into consideration your sinful nature, and the effects that nature has had on your life.

3. Your growth should be one that nurtures your spirit, soul (mind and emotions) and body. In short, it should be a balanced growth!

4. Your growth should help you interact better with others, not isolate you further from them.

5. Your growth should bring you a strong sense of inner peace.

Some Cautions

You will find many young Christians, after learning the basics of the Christian life, receiving a sense of belonging, will be compliant and wonderful to be with. You will also find others who have distinct problems, and still have many issues they must face and resolve.

The results of sin can leave devastation in our present existence, even after we have come to know Christ as Savior and Lord. There will be some who will be outright rebellious, and become the proverbial "thorn in the flesh" to the pastor, the Sunday school teacher, or anyone else who attempts to minister healing to them.

Remember every individual is unique and, consequently, their needs are unique. This is partially based on the fact they come from different family social systems which create differing beliefs, attitudes, and perceptions of the world.

We have different problems to deal with, and leaders in the Church must be willing to deal with them, regardless of how challenging they may be. God has empowered each individual in the local church with the capability of ministering to the needs of others; they only need to be willing to function fully as members of Christ's family, according to gift and maturity.

Most of the time, when we look at people, we see only the outward person, not the person's true heart. We compare what we see to the way we think people are supposed to be. Our perceptions are based upon our history, our culture, our education, and our prejudices. All these things make up our perceptual grid (the way we see the world).

We may look at people and exclaim, "Oh, Lord, they are never going to get it together, they are never going to be able to live the Christian life, they are never going to be victorious overcomers."

Some leaders will quit praying for problem believers and fellowshipping with them because "they are beyond help."

The men and women Jesus dealt with were, at times, hard-headed and hard-hearted. They had a set of belief systems entirely different from what Jesus was attempting to infuse into them. Jesus took over three years to bring change to His disciples' perception of the world, to get them ready for His Kingdom.

Even so, they did not fully understand Jesus' intentions until after Pentecost (and for some, beyond that, see Galatians 2:11-14).

We need to see others through the eyes of Christ - not as lepers, but as whole in Christ. We need to recognize they have been adopted into the wonderful family of God...where there is room for all. Until we can see people as whole, in advance of when they do truly become whole, we will inhibit them from reaching that goal.

When we pray and minister to people, focusing only on how broken they are, we will never assist them to a place where they are complete in God. Our perception of reality is not always accurate; we need to see people as Jesus sees them. We must allow God to change our hearts, letting His love permeate our perceptions.

The Wilderness Walk

The Lord has allowed me, along with all believers, a wilderness in my walk in God, bringing me to the recognition of the difference between living intimately with and without God. I quickly learned that if I did not submit to Him, and His purposes, my life would not be full. I have never doubted my salvation, but I knew I needed a deeper walk with the Lord if I was ever going to enter God's promised land for me as an individual. We all must make a similar journey.

By example, God's best for the children of Israel would have been for them to take the forty-day walk in the wilderness and go right into the Promised Land.

Young Christians, after their initial experience in Christ, do not have to forever and ever wander in the wilderness of life's problems and hurts. They do not have to take a spiritual roller-coaster ride; they do so because we leaders do not know enough to show them how to possess the land - and God's promises for them. Possessing the land is one of the goals of the healing community.

It is important to recognize that, although it was relatively easy for God to get the children of Israel out of Egypt, it was much more difficult to get Egypt out of the children of Israel. When we come to know Christ, we are translated from the kingdom of darkness to the kingdom of light; we have a new beginning and a new name. We begin the road of an intimate relationship with God. We are distinct members of a new family, with all rights and privileges.

And yet, there is still a portion of Egypt - the world's system, sin, and the results of sin - within our lives. It is required in scripture that we go through a process of change, a process that should be systematically applied to all individuals within the Body of Christ.

The Lord has provided a prescription on how to live in victory, becoming mature in God. As we begin to move from autonomy to industrious for the kingdom, and the development of a full identity based on who Jesus really is, we need to submit ourselves to the process of transformation.[2]

The Word on Healing Transformation

We find the guidance for this transformation in the book of Ephesians, beginning with Chapter 4, verse 17, and going through Chapter 5, verse 2.

> *"So I tell you this, and insist on it in the Lord, that you must no longer live as the Gentiles do, in the futility of their thinking. They are darkened in their understanding and separated from the life of God because of the ignorance that is in them due to the hardening of their hearts. Having lost all sensitivity, they have given themselves over to sensuality so as to indulge in every kind of impurity, with a continual lust for more. You, however, did not come to know Christ that way. Surely you heard of him and were taught in him in accordance with the truth that is in Jesus. You were taught, with regard to your former way of life, to put off your old self, which is being corrupted by its deceitful desires; To be made new in the attitude of your minds; And to put on the new self, created to be like God in true righteousness and holiness. Therefore each of you must put off falsehood and speak truthfully to his*

---

[2] For more on this, see Dr. DeKoven's book, *40 Days to the Promise: A Way through the Wilderness.*

neighbor, for we are all members of one body. In your anger do not sin: Do not let the sun go down while you are still angry: And do not give the devil a foothold. He who has been stealing must steal no longer, but must work, doing something useful with his own hands, that he may have something to share with those in need. Do not let any unwholesome talk come out of your mouths, but only what is helpful for building others up according to their needs, that it may benefit those who listen. And do not grieve the Holy Spirit of God, with whom you were sealed for the day of redemption. Get rid of all bitterness, rage and anger, brawling and slander, along with every form of malice. Be kind and compassionate to one another, forgiving each other, just as in Christ God forgave you. Be imitators of God, therefore, as dearly loved children; And live a life of love, just as Christ loved us and gave himself up for us as a fragrant offering and sacrifice to God." (NIV)

Let us break down what the Apostle Paul is saying. First, some context. This is a letter to the Church of Ephesus. It is important for us to remember Paul was writing to born-again, Spirit-filled Christians. These were men and women of God who, in many ways, "had it all together." They were people who loved God with all their hearts.

In the beginning of the book of Ephesians, Paul shares with them the joys of the salvation they had received, the position they have in Christ, and the great blessings of being in the family of God.

In the section just read, Paul is speaking as one who knew the people of God needed to go beyond just enjoying the benefits of being a Christian. God desires us to be transformed into the very image of Christ. In essence, Paul is stating, when we were of the world, we walked in a way that conformed to the world. We did not know God, and most of us did not care to know Him. We were ignorant, just as verse 18 describes. Our hearts were hardened; we were calloused, and all we really cared about was the fulfilling of our own needs, very much like the young child who is absorbed in his or her own self-centered aims. Our care and concern had to do with our own needs, not the needs of the family of God.

Often this pattern is true, not only with the unsaved, but with the saved as well. Further, this was a pattern of life which was true of the Greek or heathen world.

Many continue to walk carnally rather than spiritually. As Christians, we did not learn to follow Christ by worldly methods. We know Jesus Himself was not selfish. We have received the truth of who Jesus is, what great salvation He has purchased for us by the Holy Spirit. We even have an understanding of what sanctification is all about.

But, the knowledge of the truth is not enough. We must embrace and action truth to fully experience truth's benefit.

The stages of growth or transformation in character must occur within a healing community or we are destined to continue to wander in a wilderness experience. Paul's concern indicates that even Spirit-filled Christians can choose to return to old ways to living. Rather than being conformed to Christ they conform to the world. All new believers, when they receive Christ as Savior, exchange their sin-stained nature and sin-stained identity for a new identity in Christ. (They are a new creation). We are "in Christ!"

The difficult task is walking in the "new name" that comes with their adoptive status, that is, Christ in you.

Let us look further at the key verses for change. They begin with verse 22:

> *"That, in reference to your former manner of life, you lay aside the old self, which is being corrupted in accordance with the lust of deceit."*

Most believers carry into our Christian walk traumas, painful events, attitudes and beliefs of the old way of living that are contrary to God's will for us. They include our deficits, hurts and needs.

As a Christian marriage and family therapist, I have worked daily with people who have been injured or wounded severely, both in and outside of the Church. What people need more than anything else is to know there is a place where they can go and have their wounds bound and healed.

However, they also need to know they have responsibility in this healing process.

It is their responsibility to be willing to lay aside the old nature, and yield to the work of the Holy Spirit.

How is this done?

Let me suggest that God has not left us to our own devices to figure this out, nor are we bound to search for answers through humanistic psychology and philosophy. There is a process that is both good psychology and good theology found within the Word of God - we must put off the old self. That putting-off process is best described by the writer James, under the inspiration of the Holy Spirit, in James 5:16:

> *"Therefore, confess your sins to one another, and pray for one another so that you may be healed. The effective prayer of a righteous man can accomplish much."*

In proper context, the "one another" is an elder, or one mature in the Lord who can pray and keep confidences. Our faults include our character defects, our needs, and our hurts - which all must be lovingly confessed first to God.

It is also generally helpful to confess our faults, needs, and hurts to another caring human being. For most people, young Christians especially, to be willing to do that, we must create an environment in our churches that says, "We love you and accept you just the way you are." Period.

We cannot demand they become conformed to our rules, our ways and structure. This is especially true of old ways that are merely religious tradition. We must exhibit Christ's love for them. That love will generate God's power which can be released on their behalf. This, in turn, will bring about the maturing process.

Believers must be encouraged to honestly and openly begin the process of laying aside the old self. That is something we accomplish as individual Christians as we become obedient to Christ. We must present ourselves to Christ, and to the mature leadership of our Church, so the transformation process can begin.

The "putting off of the old" process is not passive; it is an active process, occurring when we make a decision of the will - a decision that says, "I will no longer live according to my old, selfish ways."

You must "violently" put away old habits, beliefs, and attitudes. However, before you can forget the past, you must remember those things that need to be forgotten. As Christians, we do not need to remember everything, or dwell on morbid details, but we do need to diligently ask the Holy Spirit, in cooperation with one or more people, to reveal to us the areas of our lives Satan has infiltrated, and where the old nature still taints.

Further, we need to put away the lies we have believed. The "lusts of deceit" really means that we are deceived by lies. The lies we still continue to believe as truth, we need to put away. We do that as the Holy Spirit reveals them to us, and as we confess one to another and to the Lord.

One good Christian lady was working through a Christian counselor to eliminate the "lusts of deceit" from her life, but was making very little progress. Each day, she desperately cried out to God to help her, and each day, she seemed to grow worse. Although she read positive, affirming truths in the Word of God, each day she continued to repeat and accept the "old lies" such as "You will never amount to anything," "You are too fat," "You are not as good as your sisters," "You will never make a good wife," etc.

Finally, one day when she was out watering the garden, her Christian husband was given a mental vision for his wife. God instructed the husband to go tell his wife the following:

"As much as you want your garden to grow, if you come out every single day and watered it with poison, only one thing would happen - the garden would die. You could pray to God to help your garden, but as long as you continued to water it each day with poison, it would die. That is what you are doing now in your spiritual growth. You are taking the garden of your mind and pouring poisonous thoughts and negative feelings upon it, and then coming to Me in prayer, asking Me to nurture your mind. Stop pouring the poison on your mind, and through My love and guidance, your mind will flourish and grow."

From that day forward, each time a negative thought would pop into the wife's mind, she would immediately label it as poison - and replace it with good nutrients - the Word of God. Today, she is a very healthy Christian lady!

Repent Through the Word

The word "repent" here means "after thought." This means nothing more than to think differently about the old ways; to think in a new way. We must be able to learn the truth of how we are to live and behave, found fully within the Word of God, and taught by responsible leadership. We then must begin to think "correctly."

This is a difficult process, but remember, we can *"do all things through Christ."*

The Word of God is clear when it says that, "For as he thinks within himself, so he is." (Proverbs 23:7). Further, *"...out of the abundance of the heart, the mouth speaks." (Matthew 12:34)*

The mind, the beliefs, the attitudes we carry within us must be challenged against the Word of God. Those things that are not a part of God's Word we need to lay aside, and allow the fruit of His Word to renew our minds.

In Romans 12:1-2, Paul says:

> *"I beseech you therefore, brethren, by the mercies of God, that ye present your bodies a living sacrifice, holy, acceptable unto God, which is your reasonable service. And be not conformed to this world: but be ye transformed <u>by the renewing of your mind</u>, that ye may prove what is that good, and acceptable, and perfect, will of God."*

The renewing of our mind comes through "the washing of the water with the Word." We must replace our old beliefs and thoughts (the way we used to see ourselves in the world), with the Word of God, God's truth, and the principles found in the Word.

Further, the Word is quick and powerful, able to bring change at the deepest part of us.

"For the word of God is quick, and powerful, and sharper than any two-edged sword, piercing even to the dividing asunder of soul and spirit, and of the joints and marrow, and is a discerner of the thoughts and intents of the heart" (Hebrews 4:12).

God's Word will reveal the truth of our hearts, and bring a dividing out of our soul, our old self, and the spirit, enabling us to walk purely before the Lord.

Finally, we must put on a new self, one created after God in righteousness and true holiness, in right thinking and right behaving. This is something we put on, that is, we need to learn to walk in a right fashion. In some ways, that means to faith it, not fake it until we make it - to walk by faith, knowing we are the righteousness of God in Christ.

Forgiveness Brings Freedom

Following repentance and confession, forgiveness needs to be received from God for real freedom from guilt and shame to occur. Forgiveness is FREELY given by God on the basis of the death of Christ, and is important for three main reasons:

1. God commands us to forgive, and our own forgiveness from God is dependent upon our willingness to forgive others.

    "For if you forgive others for their transgressions, your heavenly Father will also forgive you. But if you do not forgive others, then your Father will not forgive your transgressions." (Matthew 6:14-15).

    "Whenever you stand praying, forgive, if you have anything against anyone, so that your Father who is in heaven will also forgive you your transgressions. But if you do not forgive, neither will your Father who is in heaven forgive your transgressions." (Mark 11:25-26).

2. Forgiveness is the spiritual key to your inner healing.

"If we walk in the light, as he himself is in the light, we have fellowship with one another, and the blood of Jesus His Son cleanses us from all sin...If we confess our sins, he is faithful and righteous to forgive us our sins and to cleanse us from all unrighteousness." (1 John 1:7, 9)

3. When you fail to forgive (thus keeping the poison of resentment in your system), the person you hurt most is yourself. Be kind and compassionate to yourself. Unforgiveness binds you to the person who has hurt you. The unforgiving servant (Matthew 18:21-35) was put into prison (in our case, a mental prison) and delivered to the torturers.

Unforgiveness produces inner torment. Forgiveness releases you from your own personal negative judgments. When you forgive someone, it does not mean you approve of what the person did, but simply that you will not take God's place as their judge.

"Therefore you have no excuse, every one of you who passes judgment, for in that which you judge another, you condemn yourself; for you who judge practice the same things. And we know that the judgment of God rightly falls upon those who practice such things. But do you suppose this, O man, when you pass judgment on those who practice such things and do the same yourself, that you will escape the judgment of God?" (Romans 2:1-3)

Forgiveness, then, is a key scriptural admonition, and a key spiritual tool for your own growth.

"If your brother sins, rebuke him; and if he repents, forgive him" (Luke 17:3, NIV)

"Be kind and compassionate to one another, forgiving each other, just as in Christ God forgave you" (Ephesians 4:32, NIV)

Finally, remember forgiveness is a process; the act of forgiving moves from head to heart. The head often comes much faster than the heart, but through God's grace and guidance, complete and total forgiveness is possible. To help with this process we need:

99

a. Trusting relationships with a few people - your spouse, a good friend - who can honestly help you see blind spots you may not see.

b. When necessary, begin counseling with a competent Christian counselor. (Just as you need a physician to operate on your serious physical problems, so too, in more serious mental matters, it is almost impossible to experience total wholeness without good guidance and counseling.)

As a part of putting off the old past, we must be willing to forgive. Forgiveness is not an event; it is a process. **Lack of forgiveness is one of the greatest problems facing the Church today.**

The inability to forgive people who have hurt us in the past keeps us from moving forward in our walk with God. We must forgive, and go through the process of being set free by the power of God, not allowing bitterness to permeate our lives.

In some cases, we may need deliverance from demonic strongholds before we can continue in our growth process. This happens because unforgiveness opens the door to the demonic "tormentors."

After forgiveness, we need to know and understand the Word of God, so our minds can be renewed. The Word of God says, *"You shall know the truth and the truth will set you free."* Truth is Jesus; truth is the Word of God; truth is both a "logos" and a "rhema." We must recognize God's Word is available to all of us, because in Romans 5:8 it says:

> *"But God commendeth his love toward us, in that, while we were yet sinners, Christ died for us."*

God did not wait until we were seeking Him and trying to be good before He gave us His Son. In fact, while we were still sinful, not considering God at all, He accepted us and declared us blameless in His sight when we received Him.

Of course, God wants us to be obedient to all aspects of His Word. Paul describes obedience as the laying aside of our old self. He simply means that attitudes, contrary to Scripture, are lies that must be eliminated from our thought life.

Further, past sins of the old self must be confessed. There is a major difference between denying yourself by pretending we do not have old garbage from the past, and dealing with it. We must allow the Holy Spirit to bring our past into the light of God's Word so He can begin to change us. We do this through the process of repentance, as mentioned above. This includes the acknowledgment of the reality of that old self, and the understanding that we need to be conformed to God's plan and purposes.

"Why is it so difficult for people to go through this healing process?" you might ask.

Many people are afraid if they give up their old patterns of living they will not be able to protect themselves from being hurt. All people develop unique styles of living to meet their needs. We should show a certain respect for that. Just because someone uses drugs to get through the day, I am not going to condemn them as a horrible human being. I must ascertain what need the drugs fill. Drug use is destructive, but I know God, by His power, can deliver anyone.

The problem, as has been stated by Dr. Larry Crabb in his book *Effective Biblical Counseling*, is not so much the needs that people have, it is the strategies that they use to fulfill their needs.

For some, there is a legitimate fear in bringing to light personal needs. This fear of confession is real. As we consider confession, we need to understand its importance. The Roman Catholic Church understands this process well. We may not agree with their theology, but the concept of confession is positive. When we confess our sins to the Lord, and when we confess to a brother or sister in Christ, a cleansing occurs within us.

> *"If we confess our sins, he is faithful and just to forgive us our sins, and to cleanse us from all unrighteousness" (I John 1:9).*

When we ask another person to agree with us in prayer, we know there is great power released.

> *"Again I say unto you, That if two of you shall agree on earth as touching any thing that they shall ask, it shall be done for them of my Father which is in heaven. For where two or three*

are gathered together in my name, there am I in the midst of them" (Matthew 18:19,20).

If you share your life in prayer with someone, or confess things to them, you must have trust in their ability to keep a confidence. Sharing personal things, even with a trusted friend, is difficult for most. Because of the fear of rejection, disclosure, and ridicule, people will avoid this biblical process. Leaders must create an atmosphere of trust with their people so healthy confession can occur.

After confessing, we need to truly repent and renew our thinking in that particular area of our life. We do so by finding a specific, written Word, and meditating on it until we can put it into action.

This is a lifetime process.

It does not occur immediately.

For the Strong

Perhaps the most difficult person to minister to is the person who has been a lifelong believer. Those "born into the church," have a wonderful advantage of life-long love, nurture and care within the church. Yet, as we will see in James' teaching, even the strong need change.

James 1:21-25, says:

> *"Therefore, putting aside all filthiness and all that remains of wickedness, in humility receive the word implanted, which is able to save your souls. But prove yourselves doers of the word, and not merely hearers who delude themselves. For if anyone is a hearer of the word and not a doer, he is like a man who looks at his natural face in a mirror; for once he has looked at himself and gone away, he has immediately forgotten what kind of person he was. But one who looks intently at the perfect law, the law of liberty, and abides by it, not having become a forgetful hearer but an effectual doer, this man will be blessed in what he does."*

In this Scripture, James is writing to the Jews who have been "born again," who have a stable spiritual heritage, and yet, they must still deal with their hearts. Most came from a stable family environment, but even they needed to move beyond their comfortable foundation.

James was the primary theologian of the early Church. He writes to bring correction to Hebrew believers, especially those who must develop endurance due to the trials of their faith (James 1:2,3). He starts by admonishing them to put off filthiness and wickedness (James 1:21). Inherent in his statement is the underlying belief that filthiness and wickedness can be a part of the believer's heart. It must be put off, or cast down, so that the word of God can be received (implanted, like seed, well below the surface or pounded in) with humility. We must be willing to humble ourselves, or present ourselves to the Lord in mature behavior (Romans 12:1) for the process of change.

When James says that this process will save our souls, the salvation he is referring to is not our initial saving faith, but our continuing salvation, or our sanctification and cleansing process. As in Ephesians 4, we must submit to the process of putting off the old and renewing our mind with God's ingested Word. We must "put on the new," or act on the Word, not just think about it.

As we look in the mirror of truth, we must allow the Holy Spirit to reveal our hidden areas, then search the Word of God and apply the Word to our sins and weaknesses. Finally, we determine to act upon the truth revealed in our daily walk. The process, though difficult, does lead to freedom in Christ.
If this concept were taught and encouraged early in the Christian walk, many heartaches could be avoided. James and Paul seem to indicate a need to have this procedure become a systematic process in the Body of Christ. Rather than crisis management, we can be proactive, bringing the healing community to the Church.

A Long Process

Attitudes will change in time to line up with the Word of God. It may take a lifetime to achieve, but we should strive daily to do so. It helps to develop the daily discipline of reading and studying the Word, and further, acting upon it (James 1). More than just reading the Word, we must ingest it, devour it. When we read the Word and act upon it, it will penetrate our souls transforming our thinking.

A Life-Long Commitment

Be *"doers of the Word, not just hearers!"*

It is helpful to gather Scriptures that minister to your particular areas of need; these Scriptures will give you the faith to operate in God's power to overcome. Write these Scriptures down, memorize them, and use them, especially when the devil attacks with condemnation.

The laying off of the old, the renewing of the mind, putting on the new - are all necessary for us to be fully functional within life. To begin the process of assuming leadership, we need to have, to a significant degree, the old nature cleansed.

But it is important to remember, it is not so much the reading of the Word that makes a difference, but the doing of it daily that produces change.

It is possible to walk in His power. We do so by practicing the new self. One learning principle found in psychology is "generalization of reinforcement." The more you do something in different environments, the stronger that behavior becomes. If you are only living, responding, and behaving like a Christian at church, it is not going to help you when you go to work, or when you are in the midst of your family at home.

Learn to live the Christian life in all aspects of your world.

As we continue to traverse the process of change, laying off the old, renewing the mind, and putting on the new, God begins to change or transform our character. It is something He has promised He would do.

None of our characters are totally what they need to be, and yet, by God's grace, as we are willing to submit ourselves to His spiritual counseling process, we can begin to make changes that will be everlasting.

The Results

As we continue in Ephesians 4, we will see that Paul, after sharing the process for transformation, makes other statements of great significance. After we have submitted ourselves to the process of change, we can begin to live a life that is different.

We will begin to speak the truth.

We will begin to treat each other with equality, in fact, preferring one over the other.

Even when we are angry, we should not sin – "let not the sun go down" on our wrath. That is, we should deal with our anger face to face with the individual. We may be angry at them, but we should resolve it as soon as we can.

The devil's goal is always to divide and conquer the Body of Christ. One of the ways he does this, especially between couples, is to encourage uncontrolled anger with each other. He tries to use our own words against us to achieve his purposes.

Paul further states we should not let unwholesome words proceed from our mouths. Good examples of those unwholesome words include: "You are ugly," "I cannot stand you," "Get out of my way." These words are cruel statements, full of criticism and condemnation, words that break down the wholeness of another person, especially a member of the household of faith.

Criticism and condemnation are two of the devil's double-edged favorites.

Only words of edification, according to one's need at the moment, should be spoken. As Christians, we need to learn to speak the right word at the right time. Saying "I love you" and other words of care are going to edify and build up others in the Body of Christ.

As we go through the process of change, God will allow us to live a lifestyle that is more whole and complete in Him. Godliness is nothing more than a person's belief that we are like God, and acting in ways that emulate God's character.

Paul says that we are not to grieve the Holy Spirit of God (give the Holy Spirit a hard time by being disobedient to the Word of God).

Once you finally recognize that you are truly a child of God, you begin to understand how to appropriate the armor of God for your life.

God wants to weed out all bitterness, anger, wrath, clamor, slander, and negative concepts from our lives. As we go through the process of confession and repentance, God changes us. He helps us become loving to one another, tender-hearted, and forgiving. Once we begin to walk in this way, our lives will have far greater meaning and impact for us, and for those people we touch in our sphere of influence.

Often, pride and arrogance can keep us from submitting to God's discipling process. If we become true imitators of God, we will become like Christ. This is our goal: to remove all the weights and sin in our lives, to line up our belief systems according to God's will and purpose; to behave in a manner that displays God's principles to others.

> *"WHEREFORE seeing we also are compassed about with so great a cloud of witnesses, let us lay aside every weight, and the sin which doth so easily beset us, and let us run with patience the race that is set before us, Looking unto Jesus the author and finisher of our faith; who for the joy that was set before him endured the cross, despising the shame, and is set down at the right hand of the throne of God" (Hebrews 12:1,2)*

Once we have gone through this process, we are ready to complete the cycle of wholeness.

Questions for Discussion and Meditation

1. How can we hear God's voice more effectively? When we do, what should our response be?

2. What is the best way to minister to individuals who are attempting to fill voids in their lives inappropriately?

3. The renewing of our mind is a continuous process. How can we best keep at it and not get discouraged?

SECTION THREE

THE COMPASSIONATE LIFE

FATHERS

"I am writing to you, little children, because your sins have been forgiven you for His name's sake. <u>*I am writing to you, fathers, because you know Him who has been from the beginning.*</u> *I am writing to you, young men, because you have overcome the evil one. I have written to you, children, because you know the Father.* <u>*I have written to you, fathers, because you know Him who has been from the beginning.*</u> *I have written to you, young men, because you are strong, and the word of God abides in you, and you have overcome the evil one."*

1 John 2:12-14

CHAPTER SEVEN

DISCIPLESHIP

Jesus demonstrated God's love and concern for all mankind. He wants His body, the Church, to do the same. Just as He was involved in intimate relationships with His disciples, He wanted His disciples, in turn, to transmit this love, care, and concern to others they encountered.

We call that process discipleship.

Jesus was involved in discipling, training, and teaching men and women to know His Father. He taught them out of a "knowing" relationship with the Father. In time, they "knew" Jesus as Jesus did the Father, thus they could go out and do the works that Jesus did.

Jesus wants us, as His disciples, to use these same spiritual tools He taught His disciples for the expansion of the Kingdom today.

Those who are strong in the Lord, who have moved to a greater level of maturity, and who represent the healing community in the local church, should be willing, prepared, and available to train and lead others to a place of maturity in God.

Discipleship As Teaching

Referring back to our beloved Apostle John, he writes:

> *"I write unto you, fathers, because ye have known him that is from the beginning...I have written unto you, fathers, because ye have known him that is from the beginning" (I John 2:13a, I John 2:14a).*

This father in the faith is one who has an abiding intimacy with God as Father. To "know" here means "to know by experience." The Father has a humble maturity. His/her primary focus is on hearing the Father's voice, doing His will, and caring for the lambs and sheep.

It is only fathers and mothers that can properly bring birth and provide nurturing to little children, and guide young men and women through the wilderness experience of the Healing Community to the overcoming life. It is these who are positioned as models, teachers in the Body of Christ, mature ones who live out the compassionate life as Christ Himself did.

Teaching is an indispensable way to help others grow to maturity in the Lord; teaching is a task required of all five-fold ministers. A good teaching program will involve these vital areas:

1. There need to be prophetic voices who will proclaim or declare God's truths to others - men and women who are willing to pay the spiritual price to courageously address the hurting needs of the Body of Christ. If you are blessed with a church prophet in your local body, please pray for his/her ministry.

2. There needs to be biblical teaching on marriage and family. God created marriage, but few Christians seem to understand the sacred responsibilities of that precious sacrament. Seminars, and week-end or week-long retreats are helpful. Along with marriage, parenting training is needed. Strong biblical teaching on the family develops a healthy family system, which is vital for the survival of its members. The only way for a family to function in wholeness is to base our lives upon the principles in God's Word.

Naturally, ministry to dysfunctional families would be an offshoot of this ministry.

3. Biblical teaching on how to overcome addictive behavior is an unfortunate need today. It seems that various addictions to drugs, alcohol, sex, food, etc., have become so extensive in our society that the needs of those suffering from these addictions must be addressed as a matter of policy.

4. When needed, appropriate counseling must be available for needs in all of the above areas.

The importance of growing to full maturity in Christ is self-evident. It would be tragic if our children never separated from home to become strong, functional adults. One primary problem in new marriages occurs when a husband or wife is unable to separate from their family of origin and cleave, as the Word of God says, to their spouse (Genesis 2:24). This causes untold problems in marriages. It signals a lack of maturity.

Jesus' Type

It is interesting to study the type of people Jesus chose to be His disciples. Most of them were unlearned and untrained, certainly not theologians. But Jesus called them, just as He has called believers today, just as He has called you and me. He called them to be more than they ever thought they could be.

Just as Jesus saw potential within his disciples, He sees within us the potential for greatness we do not always see in ourselves. As Christians, and specifically as Christian leaders, we need to recognize gifts within individuals, and the wonderfulness of the people we are privileged to train for ministry.

In Romans 5:8, it says:

> *"But God demonstrates His own love toward us, in that while we were yet sinners, Christ died for us."*

God has demonstrated His love and compassion toward us while we were still sinners. It is through Christ's compassionate life that people are transformed. It was through the compassion of some ladies in the little church I attended in San Diego that I eventually bowed my knee to Christ as my Lord and Savior.

"Compassion" is the operative word, and the fundamental precept, by which Jesus ministered on earth.

This can best be illustrated in the encounter with the leper (Mark 1:40-45), which illustrates fully Jesus' compassion in the world. It reads:

> *"And a leper came to Jesus, beseeching Him and falling on his knees before Him, and saying, "If You are willing, You can make me clean." Moved with compassion, Jesus stretched out His hand and touched him, and said to him, "I am willing; be cleansed." Immediately the leprosy left him and he was cleansed. And He sternly warned him and immediately sent*

him away, and He said to him, "See that you say nothing to anyone; but go, show yourself to the priest and offer for your cleansing what Moses commanded, as a testimony to them." But he went out and began to proclaim it freely and to spread the news around, to such an extent that Jesus could no longer publicly enter a city, but stayed out in unpopulated areas; and they were coming to Him from everywhere."

In Scripture, leprosy is a symbolic representation of sin, a disease that eats away the flesh, a physical manifestation of what sin does to our souls.

It eats us away a little bit at a time.

In Christ's time, there was a prohibition against having contact with lepers. Lepers had to walk on the opposite side of the street, to cover themselves; when they came near non-infected people they would cry out: "Unclean! Unclean! Stay away!"

The man with leprosy in this scripture reference had tremendous courage!

If Jesus had been a typical religious leader of the day, He would have turned His back. To acknowledge a leper meant to identify with the sin of leprosy. But this man, sensing that he had nothing to lose, fell on his knees before Jesus and said, "If you are willing, you can make me clean."

What an interesting statement to make.

Certainly Jesus, as God, was capable of healing him! Jesus epitomized the compassion of God the Father. He went about healing the sick and casting out demons. Why wouldn't He be willing?

Yet, the question is germane today.

Are we willing? For the same question is asked of the Church today.

Compassion means "love in action."

If you say you love someone and do not give them what they need, you are deceiving yourself. Jesus was moved with compassion; He stretched out His hand and said to this leper: *"I am willing,"* and made the leper whole in body, soul and spirit. It was necessary for this man to receive Jesus' touch.

It is necessary for us as well.

Compassion Is Vital

Have you noticed that compassion is much easier with someone you know intimately? When we hear about someone's sin or problem, and we do not know them, it is easy to judge; however, if our own child or best friend falls short, or is in need, compassion is often automatic. This is why intimate relationships within the Body of Christ are absolutely necessary.

We are members of a corporate spiritual body. When one hurts, we all suffer. Compassion that has moved someone from the heart is love. The faith we need to be used by God for difficult circumstances works by love.

> *"For in Christ Jesus neither circumcision nor uncircumcision means anything, but faith working through love" (Galatians 5:6).*

We live in a society where problems are overwhelming.

Social leprosy is everywhere!

Yet, there is such hypocrisy within the Church. There are people in the Church with a certain racial heritage who are being judged wrongly because of their cultural differences, or their economic situation. People who have been divorced, people who have been abused (or have been the abusers), drug addicts, alcoholics, and former criminals might fit into this category.

Without a doubt, sin, along with its effect on the people of the world, is devastating. However, all of us are truly in the same sinful boat.

When we come to a house of worship, it should not be a mere formality. It should be a time to feed the spiritually hungry, to meet a variety of needs, to see the leper cleansed. Hurting people come to those in Christian church leadership saying, "If you are willing, you can make me whole."

Are we truly willing?

The word "whole" in the original Greek goes beyond just the physical. It involves spiritual, psychological, and physical wholeness. Jesus demonstrates that God has the ability to heal the sick and to cleanse us, thus making the entire body whole.

Today, God promises to all the opportunity to grow into wholeness, to experience wholeness through wounded healers within the walls of the healing community as the Church of Jesus Christ is moved with compassion. Jesus was moved with compassion when the leper came to Him. There were many other people with problems, but Jesus chose to help this one.

Why?

Because this man was crying out to God from his heart with a determination to receive. As Christian leaders, we need to discern in our spirits if a man is serious, if he really wants help. He or she may need some brotherly or sisterly attention, which is fine at times, or they may need true ministry.

Most people are motivated to sincerely seek help. These are the ones we need to focus on...just as Jesus did. Jesus frequently helped those who knew they had a problem and knew they needed help. When Jesus was presented with someone who had a legitimate need, He was moved with compassion, and He touched them in practical ways.

We can also touch and heal through the power of God. I am referring to more than physical miracles. I am talking about the manifestation of soul-healing. Jesus had a vision for translating His Father's love into action to reach and to reconcile the world to Himself. Jesus lived a compassionate life and so can we. It is interesting to note what happened to this leper who was cleansed. In spite of Jesus' stern request that He not spread the news, He just could not help himself. He began to go about, and as the Word of God says, he "blazed abroad the matter" - he was so on fire for God. He was so excited about what God had done he could not help but tell others about it. He may not have fully understood all he experienced in Christ, but he knew one thing for certain - he had been destined for death, but now he had life...life received through a touch from the Master's hand.

Questions for Discussion and Meditation

1. What is meant by "father's," and how must they live to affect the next generation?

2. In what way are we all lepers in need of Jesus' touch?

3. In what ways can the church and its leaders exhibit compassionate living in practical ways?

CHAPTER EIGHT

THE COMPASSIONATE RESPONSE
IN THE CHURCH

As part of leadership in a local church, one runs into people who have significant deficits in their character. Yet, at one point, they may have been, as Debbie Boone sings, "a wounded soldier who was on the front line battling for our King."

It was during the battle that they have become wounded and hurt. We, as a church, must be willing and able to minister to them in healing. I recall one incident that will help to describe what the response should be to those in Church who become wounded, whether in the Church or outside of it.

I received a call from a pastor who was in obvious distress. A couple in the church had been arrested for mutual domestic violence. The pastor received a call from the police department. The man had been arrested for abusing his wife, and she him. Both were local church leaders.

The pastor explained there was no question as to the couple's guilt, but he did not know what to do in response. The arrested man, as well as his wife, were both faithful members of the church. What no one knew, neither the couple's family nor the church, was that this had been a long term problem for them.

Of course, the pastor had some significant concerns: the reactions of the church board; the possibility of this becoming a media event; and, how it was going to affect the individuals involved.

The three typical responses of a church when faced with a crisis of this magnitude can best be illustrated in Luke 10:33-37:

> *"But a Samaritan, who was on a journey, came upon him; and when he saw him, he felt compassion, and came to him and bandaged up his wounds, pouring oil and wine on them; and he put him on his own beast, and brought him to an inn and*

*took care of him. On the next day he took out two denarii and
gave them to the innkeeper and said, 'Take care of him; and
whatever more you spend, when I return I will repay you.'
Which of these three do you think proved to be a neighbor to
the man who fell into the robbers' hands?" And he said, 'The
one who showed mercy toward him.' Then Jesus said to him,
'Go and do the same.'"*

The effects of sin had left many families in this church stripped and
beaten, emotionally and spiritually, just as the man in the parable had been
stripped and beaten.

When someone has a crisis that becomes visible, a congregation may just
bury their heads and think, "Maybe this will just go away." They choose
not to deal with it; they pretend that child abuse, incest, rape, murder,
robbery, or sins within the heart of individuals do not exist in their
community. They do not wish to believe these ugly sins exist inside the
walls of a church. They believe they have only good friends who are
absolutely wonderful people.

This is a delusion many people want to believe. In the Scripture
reference, the priest reacted to the problem by walking by on the other
side. Of course, he hoped that the situation would go away or get better
by itself.

A second response is, "Let's leave well enough alone." Just like the
Levite, who crossed the road and walked by, if you get involved, it will
only cause trouble.

This approach is a cover-up.

"Let's not disturb the status quo. Everything seems so nice and
comfortable. Why rock the boat?" This response is found in all types of
churches. People often fear if the truth comes to light, others will see
what is really within them, and judge them harshly.

Of course, we all naturally fear rejection.

But Jesus said when we are brought out of the darkness into the light, we
are to walk in the light as transformed people. Our community of
believers must be trained to recognize we are all sinners and no one is

permitted to judge one over another. We must be willing to reach out in love to the distressed soldier, and resist the temptation to shoot our wounded.

The third response is the "Let's just cut it out. Let's get this couple out of our church, let's get rid of everyone involved."

The fear here is that the problem, if known, will reflect badly on our church. Further, the problem might spread.

Do not fall for this lie of the devil!

Cutting off their support and treating them like they have leprosy will not make the situation better. Many people are not honest enough to be direct with them about their sin. We do not honestly ask them to leave, but instead withdraw from them, so they will leave "of their own accord."

As it turned out, the pastor who called had been told to deal with the situation by "cutting" their support. The governing board was very concerned about the reputation of the church. To them, saving the church meant sending the problem away because they were afraid if people found out they would no longer come to the church.

The pastor was given an ultimatum: "Get rid of this abuser or we will give you your two weeks' notice." This is not an untypical response.

Sometimes, the people of God shoot their wounded rather than work to heal them. That was the case with this church. Fortunately, to the credit of the pastor involved, he took the two weeks, rather than giving in to the pressure of that local church.

Let us look, then, at the good Samaritan.

The good Samaritan bandaged up the wounds and poured in oil for the man's healing. He did this despite the prejudices of the time. The goal, if at all possible, is to administer to hurting people forgiveness and restoration.

The victim of the church incident needed a caring family who was willing to stay with them through it; the sinner needed the same. Even in the most difficult situation, the Lord is able to meet our needs concerning the restoration of the soul.

Paul writes profoundly, in Galatians 6:1,

> *"Brethren, if a man be overtaken in a fault, ye which are spiritual, restore such an one in the spirit of meekness, considering thyself, lest thou also be tempted."*

Those of us involved in the healing community need to be willing to do four things:

1. We must be willing to take an interest in the people God brings our way. People are not perfect; they are incomplete, and may be fragmented. Sometimes, they can even be obnoxious. Yet, we need to see them as God sees them, not as they appear. They all have the potential to become men and women after God's heart. God expects us to reach out to them and administer healing, no matter how difficult the situation may seem.

2. We need to be willing and prepared to make intercession for people through communication with them, and through prayer on their behalf. One church formed a group of couples called "Shepherds." These couples had four or five new Christians assigned to them whom they took a genuine interest in, and ministered to them through prayer and fellowship.

Would it not be wonderful to know there was someone who was praying for you specifically? How reassuring it would be to know someone was watching over you in love, who was there for you for nurturing, guidance, and during times of crisis if they come.

Of course, it is difficult to minister to people when you have no idea of what their needs really are.

3. We need to be willing to make intervention, that is, to intervene when there are problems in people's lives. I do not mean an intrusionary intervention, saying or doing things against an individual's will; rather, being willing to listen and care, to give assistance and nurture, to give counsel and prayer, or to find trained resources to assist them if

necessary. This may include pastoral care and counseling, or professional assistance.

4. We need to be involved in the ministry of reconciliation. II Corinthians 5:17 says,

> *"Therefore, if any man is in Christ, he is a new creature, the old things passed away, behold, new things have come. Now all these things are from God who, reconciled us to Himself through Christ, and gave us the ministry of reconciliation."*

Paul states that God has given <u>us</u> the ministry of reconciliation, just as Jesus reconciled us. That ministry is not just to the unsaved, but to the saved as well. We need to be willing to assist in reconciling people back to a right relationship with God and each other.

Verse 19 continues:

> *"Namely, that God was in Christ reconciling the world to Himself, not counting their trespasses against them, and He has committed to us the word of reconciliation."*

It is interesting that God would call it the "word" of reconciliation.

Our goal, as members of the healing community, as we live a compassionate life, is to lead the young Christian from spiritual "toddlerhood" to spiritual maturity; to the full measure of the man or woman in Christ. We can only do this by making it our primary focus to bring healing, reconciliation, restoration, and discipleship to all men and women who are willing to be fully functional members of God's family.

We must be willing, as Christian leaders, to assist people in putting off the old natures, renewing their minds, and putting on the new selves. Then they can walk upright before the Lord. One of the ways we begin to act out the compassionate life before all people is to speak the right word to the right person, at the right time.

In closing this section on the compassionate life, let me list some of the primary concepts presenting compassion in scripture.

1. We know that compassion ruled Jesus' life. In Matthew 9:36: *"But when he saw the multitudes, he was moved with compassion on them, because they fainted, and were scattered abroad, as sheep having no shepherd."*

2. The same compassion is depicted relationally in the father's searching love for the Prodigal Son in Luke 15:20: *"And he arose, and came to his father. But when he was yet a great way off, his father saw him and had compassion, and ran, and fell on his neck, and kissed him."*

3. In Colossians 3:12, compassion is likened to a Christian hospital: *"Put on therefore, as the elect of God, holy and beloved, bowels of mercies, kindness, humbleness of mind, meekness, longsuffering;"*

4. James 5:11 says we are to be full of compassion at all times: *"Behold, we count them happy which endure. Ye have heard of the patience of Job, and have seen the end of the Lord; that the Lord is very pitiful, and of tender mercy."*

5. Concern for the poor is a working out of a compassionate life as described in Luke 4:18: *"The Spirit of the Lord is upon me, because he hath anointed me to preach the gospel to the poor."*

6. Compassion is a sacrificial love, as we find in John 15:13: *"Greater love hath no man than this, that a man lay down his life for his friends."*

7. We know that compassion or love in action edifies others: *"Now as touching things offered unto idols, we know that we have knowledge. Knowledge puffeth up, but charity edifieth"* (I Corinthians 8:1).

8. Further, love is kind: *"Charity suffereth long, and is kind; charity envieth not; charity vaunteth not itself, is not puffed up."* (I Corinthians 13:4).

9. Love is to be sought after with all of our heart because, as we know, it is not natural for us to live in a selfless, unconditional, loving way: *"Follow after charity, and desire spiritual gifts, but rather that ye may prophesy"* (I Corinthians 14:1).

10. We serve others through love or compassion: *"For, brethren, ye have been called unto liberty; only use not liberty for an occasion to the flesh, but by love serve one another" (Galatians 5:13).*

11. Part of the fruit of the Holy Spirit is love, and that love is an active love: *"But the fruit of the Spirit is love, joy, peace, longsuffering, gentleness, goodness, faith," (Galatians 5:22).*

12. The primary way we are to communicate with each other is to speak the truth in love. Just speaking the truth can be brutal; just showing love can be nothing more than sentimentality - but speaking the truth in love is the way we demonstrate God's love toward others. (Ephesians 4:25).

13. God is compassionate: *"And we have known and believed the love that God hath to us. God is love; and he that dwelleth in love dwelleth in God, and God in him" (I John 4:16).*

    "But God commendeth his love toward us, in that, while we were yet sinners, Christ died for us" (Romans 5:8).

14. Love, not just love itself, but love in action, casts out fear: *"There is no fear in love; but perfect love casteth out fear: because fear hath torment. He that feareth is not made perfect in love" (I John 4:18).*

It is important as Christians that we learn how to love one another in specific ways. We must be moved with compassion to reach out to those in need. Compassion is our primary evangelistic motivator.

In Matthew 28, Jesus' great commission states: We are to go into all the world and preach the gospel. Jesus knew that wherever the gospel was preached, wherever the good news was, transformation of life would occur.

When there is transformation of life, there is also transformation of culture, transformation of ideas, transformation of thought, and transformation of lifestyle. We need the ministry of compassion demonstrated in the Church, and the gospel of the kingdom proclaimed, motivated by love in action.

Healing Through Communion - A Final Thought

People today are looking for an experience that is real and will give meaning and purpose to their lives. As Christians, we must live a life of compassion, both with the saved and with the lost, both with those in the household of faith and with those outside.

In a church setting, receiving Holy Communion plays a very significant role in the healing process. It is clear from God's Word that the Lord's Supper involves memorial, communion, fellowship, proclamation and anticipation.

In Holy Communion, it is a chance to expose hearts - to examine ourselves as we celebrate our allegiance to Jesus. It is an action of our Christian relationship with the Lord Jesus Christ, and demonstrates our fidelity to Him. The cup reminds us Jesus loved us so much He poured out His life for us; it is for forgiveness, cleansing and healing. The cup also reminds us of the new covenant, and draws our thoughts to focus on God's love in the forgiveness of sins and the gift of the Holy Spirit.

The news that people's needs are being met - in Holy Communion and through other channels in the Church - will spread. When people's lives are touched in places they hurt the most, they cannot help but "blaze" about Jesus being real and touching lives today. This is one of the keys to a real move of God.

For the Church to go beyond developing their own comfortable intimacy with the Lord, they must reach beyond themselves, remembering where they would be without Jesus.

We must go beyond our healing, beyond a nice, comfortable fellowship; we must get back out into the world.

To live a compassionate life and to reach people where they live is our calling.

Questions for Discussion and Meditation

1. How do we handle the immature Christians who do not want to grow and change?

2. Reconciliation to God: How did it come about? What exactly does it mean to us?

3. How can we minister to other leaders whose church doors are closed to the outside, and encourage them to develop a healing ministry to the community around them?

CHAPTER NINE

DEVELOPING THE JOURNEY TO WHOLENESS IN PRACTICAL MINISTRY

As mentioned in the previous chapter, all believers are to be involved in the ministry of reconciliation bringing people back to right relationships with God. To do so, we need to be willing to cooperate fully with the Holy Spirit and His plan.

It is our responsibility as Christians to do the work of the ministry, which requires us to reach out with compassion to the world. This is illustrated by the work of the Holy Spirit, described as the Paraclete, as found in John 14:15-16:

> *"If you love Me, you will keep My commandments. I will ask the Father, and He will give you another Helper, that He may be with you forever."*

In these passages of Scripture, the Paraclete, the Holy Spirit, or the Counselor, is actively involved in bringing change. The Holy Spirit is the active agent of God in all transformation. Let's examine some of the roles of the Holy Spirit. He is...

1. The Counselor - the Holy Spirit - is likened to an intercessor. He intercedes on our behalf with groanings too great for utterance.

2. Tender and patient - the Holy Spirit - is depicted as being. As we minister in compassion, we need to be tender and patient with others.

3. Truth and leads to truth. Part of the role of the Holy Spirit, the Paraclete, the Counselor, is to reveal the truth. Truth in the inner man is necessary for us to work out our salvation "with fear and trembling."

> *"Wherefore, my beloved, as ye have always obeyed, not as in my presence only, but now much more in my absence, work out your own salvation with fear and trembling."* (Philippians 2:12).

An abiding and continuing presence; the ministry of the Paraclete is an abiding and continuing work within the believer, which is a form of discipleship. The fact is the process of change is not "a one-shot, lay your hands on, see the power of God come and knock people over" kind of ministry.

4. Our prophetic voice - The Paraclete, the Counselor, the Holy Spirit speaks with the same authority as a prophet. That authority is necessary as we war against the works of darkness.

5. Confronting believers in truth. The Holy Spirit, the Paraclete, brings people face to face with themselves, like a prosecuting attorney does, so change can occur. The goal of the Holy Spirit is to bring people to the fullness of Christ, which brings glory to God.

It is essential for leaders to be effective in ministry to those who hurt. This is a continuing ministry of every believer in the Body of Christ, as illustrated in II Corinthians 1:1-6.

> *"Paul, an apostle of Christ Jesus by the will of God, and Timothy our brother, to the church of God which is at Corinth with all the saints who are throughout Achaia: Grace to you and peace from God our Father and the Lord Jesus Christ. Blessed be the God and Father of our Lord Jesus Christ, the Father of mercies and God of all comfort, who comforts us in all our affliction so that we will be able to comfort those who are in any affliction with the comfort with which we ourselves are comforted by God. For just as the sufferings of Christ are ours in abundance, so also our comfort is abundant through Christ. But if we are afflicted, it is for your comfort and salvation; or if we are comforted, it is for your comfort, which is effective in the patient enduring of the same sufferings which we also suffer; and our hope for you is firmly grounded, knowing that as you are sharers of our sufferings, so also you are sharers of our comfort."*

6. The true Comforter, as we are to give comfort (the word "comfort" here is "paraclesis" or "counsel") to those who need care within the Body of Christ.

"Blessed be God, even the Father of our Lord Jesus Christ, the Father of mercies, and the God of all comfort; Who comforteth us in all our tribulation, that we may be able to comfort them which are in any trouble, by the comfort wherewith we ourselves are comforted of God." (II Corinthians 1:3,4)

In doing so, we function in similar fashion to a wise counselor or advisor found in the Old Testament. As we cooperate fully with the Holy Spirit, we will assist people to become all that God created them to be.

Questions for Discussion and Meditation

1. What is the role of the Holy Spirit for believers?

2. How can we cooperate more fully with the Holy Spirit in the transformation of lives?

CHAPTER TEN

SPECIAL LEADERSHIP CHALLENGES

This chapter is written primarily to those who are in leadership, or who desire to be leaders, and to those in positions of influence within the Church.

As a member of the Church, which represents the Body of Christ, you must ascertain what your people need. To discover those needs, you must become actively involved in their lives. Typically, people do not openly volunteer to share their needs. In relationships, just as in seeking after God, people often function as if they have blinders over their eyes.

Make "learning the needs" within your local church body an active policy so the *Journey to Wholeness* will develop. All needs within the Body of Christ are important: emotional, psychological, physical, vocational, financial, and spiritual. A ministry team with a learned leader needs to be developed to meet the various needs within the Body.

After the Assessment

In light of the journey that all of us are on, it is essential to assess where individuals and churches are in their spiritual walk. Without a clear picture, we often "shoot in the dark," missing the mark of the needs of God's people.

First, you must know the spiritual history of your congregation. What has their foundation been like? Have they been systematically trained, do they know how to worship, etc.? We often assume when we should not. *"If the foundations be destroyed, what can the righteous do?" (Psalm 11:3).* Only God, the Holy Spirit, and God's Word can restore the broken foundation.

Second, have your people been through a time of healing? What problems, needs, hurts, and other damage exists? Have they ever taken the "journey within," led by the Holy Spirit, to bring healing and wholeness? If not, the need for ministry is clear.

Finally, do you have compassionate activity in your membership? Are evangelism, care for the poor, and pastoral care for the hurting part of your fellowship? The answers to these questions will help lead to the overall direction for the individual and the church.

Remember, there will always be a percentage of new converts and struggling souls. Our hope is to make these people mature and develop to fulfill their destiny, and turn them into compassionate servants for others.

Leadership Choices

For a given ministry need, a leader should be chosen from the congregation by God through the pastoral leadership. Very rarely do people with no inkling of a need hear a clear voice from the Lord telling them to be involved in ministry. So, as a group, the church leadership prays for a man or woman that God directs to be in charge of a certain ministry function.

Simultaneously, the Lord will begin to speak to the right person's heart concerning the needs of the people. That person is then confirmed by the pastoral leadership. It is not to be done by election, vote, talent, or time, but by the Holy Spirit.

In His perfect timing, God will raise up just the right person for leadership.

If God has put a desire in an individual's heart for a certain ministry, but that ministry is not needed at the present time, it does not mean that person should search out a different church. They may need to wait, and at the right time, God will bring that particular ministry to pass.

In Australia, Christians are in sufficient submission to the pastoral leadership that they may wait for years before they set forth into ministry. They wait until it is clear from the Holy Spirit...then they are sent forth with greater results.

If you have a burden for ministry but do not have skills, learn about it. Talk to others who are successful in ministry, and have similar callings. There is no reason for you to re-do what others have already done. It is best to synthesize all the available information regarding the accomplishments of a particular ministry, then develop a program suited to the unique needs of your fellowship.

After need and leadership are chosen, it is necessary to recruit helpers who will have the ability and a **vision** for the same goal.

In Scripture, the leader always has helpers. You will find helpers, first of all by communicating the need to the congregation, and then, asking the Lord to bring the people who are finally confirmed by leadership.

As a leader, or potential leader, you need to plan your ministry with care, and with a view to the future. As leaders, we think in terms of finding our replacement. There is no place in the Body of Christ for power struggles and politics. We cannot afford to waste our time when there are so many hurting people in need.

Your job is to make your area of ministry "extinct." All too often, we develop programs or ministries with an attempt to hang on to them beyond their usefulness. Then, it becomes a "my ministry" struggle, not a ministry ordained by God.

If a ministry is not ordained by God, then why be in it?

After finding helpers, a process group needs to be developed. This group should have regular meetings where it develops and reevaluates ministry needs. It will ask questions like "Is the ministry still being effective to meet the needs of the people?"

All too often we fail to evaluate what we are doing. Maybe the ministry just needs modifications; nothing in the Body of Christ should be taken for granted. It is human nature to resist change, but it is vitally important that change be allowed where necessary. Everything done within a group to reach out and develop healing or encourage people's gifts needs to be encouraged for God's glory.

Reflections

Let us examine more closely the process necessary to achieve a compassionate Christian walk, focusing on how we, as leaders, can bring God's people to this level of maturity.

New converts want to fit into the family of God. We all must have instilled within us a sense of belonging. This is especially true for all who have experienced rejection within their family. Just being included in God's family, in and of itself, is quite healing.

People have such a need to belong, to be wanted, appreciated, and loved. Our People should sense the love of God and the people around them. They should know they fit in, feel at home, they belong. That is the goal for our spiritual children!

Remember there must be a certain amount of freedom, discipline, and, of course, unconditional love for children to grow. It is your responsibility, as leadership, to provide the atmosphere of family, to teach and integrate them into the family of God. We need to be a part of a community of faith that is alive and vibrant.

Ephesians 4:1, NIV, says:

> "I urge you to live a life worthy of the calling you have received."

All believers must know who they are in Christ.

One thing that Jesus wants for us, as He renews our minds, is to help us know who we are in Him. We are the righteousness of God in Christ. This is one of the many new "I am" messages that is given to us in the Word of God.

We have discussed in this book about the process of putting off the old, renewing our mind, and putting on the new (Ephesians 4:17-32). In Ephesians 5:1-2 we are used to imitate Christ and to become just like Him.

> *Therefore be imitators of God, as beloved children; and walk in love, just as Christ also loved you and gave Himself up for us, an offering and a sacrifice to God as a fragrant aroma.*

In the entire Book of Ephesians, Paul is addressing the Church. The Church was Paul's passion, he loved the Church and the precious people of God.

Today, as in Paul's day, there are many who are still livi[ng] beneath their inheritance, without fulfilling their God-ordained purpose.

There are many churches where people are saved, sanctifie[d] [fil]led with the Holy Spirit, yet, still sit in their seats week after week, ne[ver gr]owing or changing. As Christians, we may experience similar stagn[ation] that of the children of Israel. We stall in the wilderness rather than [...] enter God's promises.

Paul admonished us to be careful of developing a hard heart, [...] inappropriate sensuality and to grow in God's prosperity.

Of course, there is a difference between godly prosperity and w[...] prosperity.

The Lord blesses us because of what Jesus did and, as we walk in close relationship with Him, He will meet our needs.

> *"That he would grant you, according to the riches of his glory,*
> *to be strengthened with might by his Spirit in the inner man"*
> *(Ephesians 3:16).*

He meets physical needs as well as spiritual needs -- as long as we live according to His principles.

As leaders, we encounter people who do not understand these principles. They resisted Jesus; they resisted Paul; they will resist us. Our response is to continue to challenge people with the truth of God's conforming power, trusting God for the end result.

Paul wanted the church to go on to maturity, into that place called the "Promised Land," to bring people to rest in God, fulfilling their lives and callings in Him. Our focus should be no less, and our compassionate action should be to do all we can, as God gives us strength, to help our charge become all that God intended, for His glory.

CHAPTER ELEVEN

THE COMPASSIONATE LIFE: MOVING BEYOND THE CHURCH

The ultimate goal in our *Journey to Wholeness* is not to get people to a place where they are just healed and self-sufficient within the Body of Christ.

The goal for the Body of Christ is not to just receive personal blessings and enjoy wonderful times; rather, we are healed, restored, and blessed to take this Good News of Christ to the world.

The Lord chose a very simple people to fulfill His purposes. They had a heart toward God and had received a radical call from a radical Christ.

In the natural, we may not have chosen the people that Jesus selected.

In reality, there are times when we do not particularly care for the ones God has brought to our fellowship; yet, it is so vital to learn to love them where they are, and provide a way for them to become all that God created them to be.

As a leader of people, we must work with the ones God has brought to us. People are a blessing from God, and it should be our purpose to work with them. Developing intimate relationships is absolutely necessary for a productive, healing community. We need to minister to our community and look at how we can meet needs outside of the Church.

We must ask the question, "What can we do?" How can we bring a cup of water "in the Name of Jesus"?

Jesus spent time in the temple during His earthly ministry. But He spent the majority of His time with the people in the world.

All too often church members, and leadership within the Church, spend their energy trying to keep people in the Church, so we only give them ministry tasks only within our four walls. We act afraid to send people out to do work for the Lord.

That was not the concern of Jesus or Paul. They concerned themselves with finding enough people to send out.

Anyone sent out, or who goes out on their own, must move out in love, seeking from the heart of God ways to meet the needs of their community. By "going out," I am not necessarily talking about overseas ministry. Most churches already participate in supporting missionaries overseas. We need to "go out" and infiltrate our neighborhoods, getting involved in the lives of those around us. If a person is not actively involved in the process of reaching others for Christ, they are missing on a great blessing.

Just as we need to experience times of healing within ourselves, we need to be able to offer that healing to a lost and dying world. Remember, as Christians, we are not satellites unto ourselves. We must continue to develop our relationship with God, and remain dependent upon Him.

Although we must be connected to others in the Body of Christ, we should be less dependent upon people as we grow and change. In psychology, this is what is meant by "separation and individuation," a process by which a child moves from being totally dependent upon Mom and Dad, to becoming independent.

For a long time it was assumed identity was completed by the age of eighteen. However, recent research has indicated it is not completed until the age of 30. It is interesting to note Jesus waited until He was 30 before He began His ministry.

We need to bring people to a level of maturity that breeds independence, and yet, the ultimate goal of interdependence must be accomplished with other members of the Body of Christ, while reaching out to a lost and dying world.

A compassionate life is one of moving out into the world with a heart for ministry. Any church that is involved in only taking care of their own friends and members is not fulfilling the whole counsel of God. It is absolutely essential that we fulfill the great commission. Jesus tells us to go into all the world and preach the gospel and make disciples.

This gospel - the gospel of hope and healing, the gospel of salvation - changes nations. It is the best way to bring about change within Third World countries.

As people begin to live according to biblical principles, their entire way of seeing the world, and their way of living will change.

Too often we give up on people when problems are not immediately solved with minimal efforts. We must learn to be long-suffering. When Jesus ministered, He counted the cost, but was still moved by compassion for the needs of people. He did not worry about their spiritual condition only.

Jesus met both their physical and emotional needs!

It is part of God's character, and one of the components of His nature, to be a God of love and compassion.

In Colossians 3:12, NIV, it says:

> *"Therefore as God's chosen people, holy and dearly loved, clothe yourselves with compassion, kindness, humility, gentleness and patience."*

To live in a compassionate manner is a command. Demonstration of compassion is evidenced by a special love for the less fortunate, the poor, the widowed, the orphan, the elderly. There are widows and widowers, some caused by death, and some by divorce. We call divorced people "single," not "widows and widowers," yet the dramatic separation process they experience is often much closer to suffering the loss of a loved one through death. The loss is almost identical, but actually, in a divorce it is a bit more difficult because the corpse is still walking around. The feelings and the needs are still the same. God has a special place in his heart for the widowed, the orphaned, and the poor, as we see in Psalm 34:18:

> *"The LORD is nigh unto them that are of a broken heart; and saveth such as be of a contrite spirit."*

The life of compassion is self-sacrificing, just as Jesus was the primary sacrifice for us all.

We must serve people from a heart of compassion.

Most in the Body of Christ know they are loved by God. The world needs to know the love of God, as demonstrated by our love for one another. We need to model His love for us. We need to model the fruit of the Holy Spirit in our lives. In the fruit of the Spirit, love is primary.

Love that reaches out and touches is a love in action, not just words.

Finally, compassion and true love cast out fear. Fear and love cannot mix together; neither can faith and fear mix. If you are ministering in love, there is no need for fear. This form of compassion, alive and active, must not just be preached from the pulpit, but acted out in pastoral response.

Our actions do speak much louder than words.

Finally, let me list four keys to a compassionate life.

1. As an effective care-giver, the primary attribute that is necessary to live a compassionate life is **the ability to express empathy**, the ability to see someone from their viewpoint. Liking someone is not a prerequisite for being able to feel their pain.

   A counselor or care-giver must seek to understand how a person feels and what they are thinking, whether they are members of the Body of Christ or not. God wanted to know us so intensely that He became one of us.

   Empathy is best communicated in non-verbal ways, by the way we act, and the manner in which we listen. This is called "active or reflective" listening; it communicates understanding to the other person.

   A good Scripture in support of this is Proverbs 12:25, NIV:

   "An anxious heart weighs a man down, but a kind word cheers him up."

Even while Jesus was dying on the cross He was able to identify with the pain of the dying prisoner and reached out to him with hope and salvation.

2. If you desire to be a compassionate care-giver, you must have the ability to show **warmth or mercy** (Romans 5:8; Luke 10:30-37).

    Warmth is a caring love usually communicated non-verbally. Warmth is the understanding nod of the head, the listening ear, the holding of the hand, and eye contact with people. The eyes are the windows of the soul - look into their eyes with the love of the Holy Spirit.

    People will feel God's warmth, not only by our words, but also by our actions - actions in the best interest of the other.

3. The care-giver should show **respect**. The root word for "respect" is "to see" or "to view." We must see someone as valuable, prizing them simply because they are human beings. As we show respect toward others, God will lift them toward His image of them.

    Self-esteem, or a positive self-image, is given to children as they grow. One of the ways to raise someone's self-image is to show them respect. You respect someone by prizing them. Respect is an attitude of the heart which is demonstrated by our actions. We must orient ourselves toward others, and show honor and reverence, treating them as our equal.

    An excellent example of respect is provided in the biblical accounts of how Jesus treated people. Against all conventions, Jesus treated the lowly with respect. He especially showed respect to women. He spent most of His time with those who were considered "less than" others. Once I heard a pastor declare, "The way we reflect our Christianity is by how we treat the powerless people in our lives." He defined "powerless people" as "those who could do nothing for us."

    That is so true. If you treat the man who sweeps your office with the same respect you treat your boss, then you are well on your way to living as Christ lived!

4. We need to be **trustworthy**. In Proverbs 11:13, NIV, and Proverbs 13:3, NIV, we see a description of our need to be trustworthy.

"A gossip betrays a confidence, but a trustworthy man keeps a secret. He who guards his lips guards his life, but he who speaks rashly will come to ruin."

It is very important we be aware of the need for confidentiality in our dealings with people. We may remember times when we have shared "a secret" with someone, even a pastor, only to hear our story illustrated in the next Sunday service.

That is not the way it should be.

Being trustful, warm, empathetic, and respectful are keys to ministry if you wish to be effective with people.

My Prayer for You

We have looked in depth at the development, and our process of growth, line upon line, precept upon precept. The purpose has been to provide a clear description of the process we must go through to become whole as God's people, and to assist others to become the servants of God that they wanted to be. To be whole and complete in Him means to be genuine Christian people.

The world will know we are Christians by our love. As we fulfill the Great Commission, living a compassionate life, continuing to walk in intimate relationship with the Lord, allowing the Lord to daily transform us into the image of His own dear Son, Jesus, the world will know we are His.

My prayer is that you will fulfill all righteousness for your life, continue your journey, fulfill your call, and help others do the same along their *Journey to Wholeness.*

BIBLIOGRAPHY

Bradshaw, J.; The Family. Deerfield Beach, FL: Health Comm. Inc.; 1988: 6, 20.

Chant, Dr. Ken; The Christian Life, Vision Publishing, Ramona, CA, 1988.

Collins, Gary; How to be a People Helper. Vision House Publishing., 1976.

Crabb, Lawrence Jr.; Effective Biblical Counseling. Grand Rapids: Zondervan; 1977: 129.

Dalbey, G.; Healing the Masculine Soul. Waco: Word Books; 1988: 27.

DeKoven, Dr. Stan, *40 Days to the Promise*, Vision Publishing, Ramona, CA, 1993.

DeKoven, Stan, *Fresh Manna: How to Study the Word*. Vision Publishing, Ramona, CA, 2000.

DeKoven, Stan. *I Want to Be Like You, Dad*. Vision Publishing, Ramona, CA, 1996.

DeKoven, Stan, *Marriage and Family Life*, Vision Publishing, Ramona, CA, 1990.

DeKoven, Dr. Stan, New Beginnings: A Sure Foundation, Vision Publishing, Ramona, CA, 1990.

Dobson, J.; Love Must Be Tough. Dallas: Word Pub.; 1983.

Dobson, J.; Straight Talk to Men and Their Wives. Waco: Word Books; 1980: 22-23.

Freedman, Edwin; Generation to Generation. New York: Guidford Press; 1982: 1.

Gill, A.L., Praise and Worship: A Study Guide, Powerhouse Publishing, Fawnskin, CA.

Kaufman, Dr. Gerald; It's Time For War: Warfare Prayer. Logos International Publishing Company; 1988.

Miller, Keith; Sin: Overcoming The Ultimate Deadly Addiction. San Francisco: Harper and Row, 1987.

Payne, Leanne; The Healing Presence. Westchester: Crossway Books, 1989. 128,129.

Sanford, John and Paul; Transformation of the Inner Man. Tulsa: Victory House, 1982: 277,278.

Seamands, David; Healing for Damaged Emotions. Wheaton: Victor Books, 1986: 79.

Seamands, David; Putting Away Childish Things. Wheaton: Victor Books, 1982: 10.

Sweeten, Gary; Rational Christian Thinking. Cincinnati: Equipping Ministry International, 1988.

* * *

Other Helpful Books by Dr. DeKoven on related topics include:

- *On Belay! Introduction to Christian Counseling*
- *Catch the Vision*
- *Family Violence: Patterns of Destruction*
- *Turning Points: Ministry in Crisis Times*
- *Forty Days to the Promise: A Way Through the Wilderness*
- *Marriage and Family Life: A Christian Perspective*
- *I Want to Be Like You, Dad: Breaking Free from Generational Patterns-Restoring the Heart of the Father*
- *Parenting on Purpose*
- *Keys to Successful Living*
- *Fresh Manna: How to Study the Word*
- *New Beginnings*

About the Teaching Ministry
of Dr. Stan DeKoven

Dr. DeKoven conducts seminars based upon his books in his "Walk in Wisdom" seminar program. As an outreach of the Vision Christian University Bible College Network and the Family Care Network Counseling Ministry, Dr. DeKoven brings fresh and anointed insights for practical Christian living through biblical revelation. The focus of his ministry is restoration and preparation. Each seminar is designed to bring restoration and healing to the Body of Christ and preparation for greater service in the Church and beyond. To contact Dr. DeKoven, please write to:

Walk in Wisdom
c/o Vision Publishing
1520 Main Street, Suite C
Ramona, CA 92065
(760) 789-4700
www.visionpublishingservices.edu

About the Author

Stan E. DeKoven, Ph.D., is a licensed Marriage, Family and Child Therapist in San Diego, California, and a certified School Psychologist. Dr. DeKoven received his Bachelors degree in Psychology from San Diego State University, his Masters in Counseling from Webster University, and his Ph.D. in Counseling Psychology from the Professional School of Psychological Studies. He has also completed a Bachelors and Masters in Theology, and his Doctorate in Ministry from Evangelical Theological Seminary.

He is Founder and President of Vision Christian Ministries and Vision Christian University. Dr. DeKoven has been a family counselor in private and group practice for over twelve years.

His special concerns include: Counselor education, family violence, substance abuse, and Bible College Development. He is President of The Family Care Network, and has been a pastor for several years.

Dr. DeKoven is married to his beautiful wife Noreen, and has two daughters, Rebecca and Rachel.

Journey to Wholeness:
Discipleship Program

Looking for a teaching program to lead your converts/congregants to responsible maturity in Christ?

Dr. DeKoven's Journey to Wholeness Discipleship Program may be what you are looking for.

Included in this program is:

- *New Beginnings: First Steps in Christ*
- *Fresh Manna: How to Study the Word*
- *40 Days to the Promise: A Way Through the Wilderness*
- *Marriage and Family Life*
- *Journey to Wholeness*

LaVergne, TN USA
30 April 2010
181126LV00004B/46/A